Classic
CROCHETED VESTS

Classic
CROCHETED VESTS

Nancie M. Wiseman

Martingale®
& C O M P A N Y

Credits

President • Nancy J. Martin
CEO • Daniel J. Martin
Publisher • Jane Hamada
Editorial Director • Mary V. Green
Managing Editor • Tina Cook
Technical Editor • Ursula Reikes
Copy Editor • Liz McGehee
Design Director • Stan Green
Illustrator • Laurel Strand
Cover and Text Designer • Shelly Garrison
Fashion Photographer • John P. Hamel
Photographer's Assistant • T. J. Gettings
Fashion Stylist • Susan Huxley
Hair and Makeup • Lori Smith
Studio Photographer • Brent Kane

Classic Crocheted Vests
© 2004 by Nancie M. Wiseman

Martingale & Company
20205 144th Avenue NE
Woodinville, WA 98072-8478 USA
www.martingale-pub.com

Printed in China
09 08 07 06 05 04   8 7 6 5 4 3 2 1

Library of Congress Cataloging-in-Publication Data

Wiseman, Nancie M.
    Classic crocheted vests / Nancie M. Wiseman.
        p. cm.
    Includes bibliographical references.
    ISBN 1-56477-543-7
    1. Crocheting—Patterns. 2. Vests. I. Title.
    TT825.W575 2004
    746.43'40432—dc22

                                    2004012855

Mission Statement
Dedicated to providing quality products and
service to inspire creativity.

Acknowledgments

It always gives me great pleasure to acknowledge the special people in my life who allow me the time and give me the encouragement to write books.

To my husband, Bill Attwater, who is always first on the list. He's the greatest guy—he cooks, cleans, and basically does everything. He's a great encouragement and the love of my life.

To my grandma Bessie, who taught my mother, Thayes, to do needlework, who then taught me. Thank you both for starting me on my way with crochet, knitting, and needlework so many years ago. I didn't know my grandma, but I feel she played a big part in my receiving all of my handwork skills from my mom. I thank them both so much for taking a tiny little girl and planting the seed for needlework in her brain and giving her a skill to love and to follow passionately. I believe that it takes true passion and love to take a beloved craft and learn it, teach it, and then write about it. Again, thank you so much!

To the folks at Martingale & Company, I can never thank you enough for trusting me with another book; it is always a pleasure to work with you—especially my technical editor, Ursula Reikes, who is steadfast and even-tempered through it all, even when my brain is ready to say "Enough!" Ursula is always there with great ideas and good humor, even when we have to solve problems while I'm sitting in an airport. A terrific editor and a good friend, she's the true believer and the unsung hero of these books.

And of course, to you, the reader, who continues to devour books for every possible tidbit of information you can glean from the pages. I am always appreciative of you and your comments. It's for you these books are written and why we work so hard to make them as perfect as we can. I hope you enjoy every word and every design!

Contents

Thayes and four-year-old Nancie with their needlework

Introduction

My mother was always crocheting, knitting, or sewing. Although I don't remember being taught how to do any of it, somehow it all became a part of my life. It seems that I could always read a pattern and crochet or knit without giving it much thought.

When I look at my hands as I crochet, it is like seeing my mother's hands as I watched her crochet when I was a kid: the same age spots, the same crooked index finger on our right hands. We even hold the hook the same way! It's amazing to me that those skills just seemed to come to me "with the territory," so to speak. I guess while sitting by her side for all those years I must have learned by watching. Believe me, you never sat in my mother's living room without doing something in the evening. Even my brothers used to sew a little and do "stuff," as my brother Charlie says.

As my mother aged, she quit following written crochet patterns and preferred instead to work from the pictures that came with the patterns. She loved doilies and bedspreads and particularly the ripple afghan and the pineapple doily. My brothers and I all received loads of each of them.

In her later years, when Mom would get stuck with the ripple pattern in an afghan, she would call me at my shop, Nancie Knits, and ask if I could help her. She would usually say she had gotten stuck at the bottom of the "hill" and couldn't remember how to get back to the "top of the hill." If you're not familiar with this pattern, see Ripples on page 80. It was hard for me to believe that she needed help because she had made so many of those afghans, but it was also fun for me to be able to help her for a change.

When I decided that *Classic Crocheted Vests* would be a great book to follow *Classic Knitted Vests* (Martingale and Company, 2003), I set out to design interesting and fun vests that crocheters would enjoy making and wearing. There are basic, traditional vests made with traditional yarns, and some made with fun yarns that do the "talking." There are patterns that include different shaping as well as color work. Some are just plain fun to crochet, and one or two may even challenge your brain a bit.

I hope you'll find some vests that fit your lifestyle and level of crochet. I've included some "how to" information as it applies to each vest as well as some general information that applies to all of the vests and crochet in general. There are also some new guidelines, adopted by the Craft Yarn Council of America, which have been integrated into the patterns. All of your questions should be answered right here in this book. So don't hesitate. Pick your first project, take a trip to your local yarn shop, buy some yarn, and sit right down and make that first gauge swatch!

New Standards for Crochet

Recently the Craft Yarn Council of America, which is made up of several yarn companies, pattern manufacturers, hook and needle manufacturers, magazines, and needlework organizations, agreed to set certain standards for labeling yarn and hook and needle sizes. These guidelines are meant to make buying yarn, reading patterns, and choosing hooks and needles easier. It will take a while for all of this to become commonplace, but it is certainly a step forward to making the process easier when we dive into a project. I have included some of the new symbols in the patterns so that you can become familiar with these.

CROCHET HOOKS

This is an abbreviated list of the crochet-hook equivalents. All hook sizes will be listed in U.S. sizes and metric sizes. The millimeter size is the most accurate for sizing the hooks; the letter or number on the U.S. sizes may vary from manufacturer to manufacturer.

Size in Millimeters	U.S. Size Range
2.25	B-1
2.75	C-2
3.25	D-3
3.5	E-4
3.75	F-5
4	G-6
4.5	7
5	H-8
5.5	I-9
6	J-10
6.5	K-10½
8	L-11
9	M/N-13

SKILL LEVELS

There are new definitions and symbols for skill levels.

■□□□ **Beginner:** Projects for first-time crocheters using basic stitches. Minimal shaping.

■■□□ **Easy:** Projects using yarn or thread with basic stitches, repetitive stitch patterns, simple color changes, and simple shaping and finishing.

■■■□ **Intermediate:** Projects using a variety of techniques, such as basic lace patterns or color patterns, midlevel shaping, and finishing.

■■■■ **Experienced:** Projects with intricate stitch patterns, techniques, and dimension, such as nonrepeating patterns, multicolor techniques, fine threads, small hooks, detailed shaping, and refined finishing.

STANDARD YARN-WEIGHT SYSTEM

The new yarn labeling system utilizes a number to represent the weight of the yarn and the size hook to use with it. The chart below gives an abbreviated version of the labeling system as it applies to crochet.

Yarn-Weight Symbol and Category Names	1 SUPER FINE	2 FINE	3 LIGHT	4 MEDIUM	5 BULKY	6 SUPER BULKY
Types of Yarns in Category	Sock, Fingering, Baby	Sport, Baby	DK, Light Worsted	Worsted, Afghan, Aran	Chunky, Craft, Rug	Bulky, Roving
Crochet Gauge Ranges in Single Crochet to 4"	21 to 32 sts	16 to 20 sts	12 to 17 sts	11 to 14 sts	8 to 11 sts	5 to 9 sts
Recommended Hook in Metric Size Range	2.25 to 3.5 mm	3.5 to 4.5 mm	4.5 to 5.5 mm	5.5 to 6.5 mm	6.5 to 9 mm	9 mm and larger
Recommended Hook in U.S. Size Range	B-1 to E-4	E-4 to 7	7 to I-9	I-9 to K-10.5	K-10.5 to M-13	M-13 and larger

For complete information on all of the changes the Craft Yarn Council of America and all of its affiliates are making, refer to the Web site www.yarnstandards.com.

Hints and Tips for Better Crochet

Crochet has always been known as easy to fudge. It seems that if you didn't have the right amount of stitches you could just skip a stitch or add a stitch and it wouldn't matter too much. Well, my friend, I'm here to tell you that there are times when you can do that, but I don't recommend it. Many stitch patterns have a multiple that must be worked over a certain number of stitches. If you no longer have the number of stitches for your pattern to work correctly, the best thing to do is just rip out the stitches and get back to the correct number of stitches.

It's helpful to have an understanding of the stitches and the patterns so that if you do happen to find a mistake it is a little easier to figure out what to do. Making a gauge swatch will give you a feel for the pattern as well as the yarn. As you work the swatch, do your best to visualize what is happening in the pattern and why you are told to do certain things. Don't just merrily crochet along without trying to understand. Look at your work and see what is occurring and how the pattern is forming. This will help you spot errors more quickly when you look at the work and all of a sudden see something out of place. And by all means, rip out the mistake! I know, I hate to rip too, but if it bothers you now, it will continue to bother you. You'll end up pointing it out to people and saying to yourself "Why didn't I rip that out and fix it?" Come on, you know what I'm talking about, right?

Let me try and help you understand what is happening and where some of the mistakes are occurring. I don't mind fixing mistakes when I know what happened.

BACK

- Ch 99 (111, 123, 135), sc in 2nd ch from hook and in each ch across—98 (110, 122, 134) sts. **Next 3 rows:** Ch 1, sc in each st across, turn.

- Work foundation row, then work row 1 of patt st until piece measures 8 (8, 9, 10)", end with completed WS row, turn.

- **Armholes:** Sl st across 13 (13, 16, 19) sts, ch 2 (count as dc), work in patt to last 12 (12, 15, 18) sts, turn. Work armhole dec as follows: **Row 1:** Ch 2 (count as dc), work dc2tog in first ch-1 sp at beg of row, work in patt to last ch-1 sp, dc2tog in last ch-1 sp, dc in tch, turn. **Row 2:** Ch 2 (count as dc), sk next ch-1 sp, work in patt to last ch-1 sp, sk ch-1 sp, dc in tch, turn. These 2 rows eliminate 3 sts at each end of the work. Rep these 2 rows once more—62 (74, 80, 86) sts. Cont in patt until armhole measures 9 (10, 10, 11)".

- **Right shoulder:** Ch 2 (count as dc), *(dc, ch 1, dc) in next ch-1 sp, rep from * 3 (4, 5, 6) more times. Fasten off.

- **Left shoulder:** With RS facing, reattach yarn in ch-1 sp 4 (5, 6, 7) from left, ch 3 (counts as dc and ch-1 sp), dc in same sp, cont in patt to end of row. Fasten off.

LEFT FRONT

- Ch 117 (123, 129, 135) sts, work as for back until 2 rows of patt st have been completed—116 (122, 128, 134) sts.*

- Work in patt over first 53 (59, 65, 71) sts only. Leave rem sts to be completed later for tie.

- Cont in patt until piece measures 8 (8, 9, 10)", end with completed WS row, turn.

- **Armhole shaping:** Sl st across 13 (13, 16, 19) sts, ch 2 (count as dc), work in patt to end, turn. Work armhole dec as follows: **Row 1:** Work in patt to last ch-1 sp at armhole edge, work dc2tog in last ch-1 sp, dc in tch, turn. **Row 2:** Sk next ch-1 sp at armhole edge, cont in patt to end, turn. Rep these 2 rows once more—35 (41, 44, 47) sts. Cont in established patt until armhole measures same as back, end with completed RS row.

- **Neck shaping and collar:** Work in patt across next 21 (24, 24, 24) sts, dc in next dc. Leave rem 13 (16, 19, 22) sts unworked for shoulder. Cont in patt until collar measures 1" longer than one-half of back neck, approx 4¼ (4⅝, 4⅝, 4⅝)". Fasten off.

RIGHT FRONT

- Work as for left front to *. Fasten off.

- Counting from left to right, with RS facing, reattach yarn at st 53 (59, 65, 71), ch 2 (count as dc), work in patt to end.

- Cont in patt until work measures 8 (8, 9, 10)", end with completed WS row.

- **Armhole shaping:** Work in patt to last 12 (12, 15, 18) sts, turn. Work armhole dec as follows: **Row 1:** Ch 2 (count as dc), work dc2tog in first ch-1 sp at armhole edge, cont in patt to end, turn. **Row 2:** Work in patt to last ch-1 sp at armhole edge, sk last ch-1 sp, dc in tch, turn. Rep these 2 rows once more—35 (41, 44, 47) sts. Cont in patt until armhole measures same as back, end with completed RS row. Fasten off.

- **Neck shaping and collar:** With WS facing, reattach yarn to st 14 (17, 20, 23) from end, ch 2 (count as dc), work in patt across next 21 (24, 24, 24) sts. Cont until collar measures same as left front. Fasten off.

Finishing

- With pieces flat and RS facing up, whipstitch shoulder seams tog.

- Whipstitch finished ends of collar tog with RS facing.

- Pin collar to back neck, easing to fit, and whipstitch into place with WS tog.

- Weave side seams tog.

- **Left front tie:** With RS facing, attach yarn at beg of body edge of tie, ch 1, sc into each st across, turn. Rep from * for 3 more rows. Fasten off. Sew new rows of band to edge of body.

- **Right front tie:** Work as for left front, beg at outer end of tie with RS facing. Sew new rows of band to edge of body.

- Mist with water and lay flat to dry. Be careful not to stretch out the front or armhole edges since no borders are added to them.

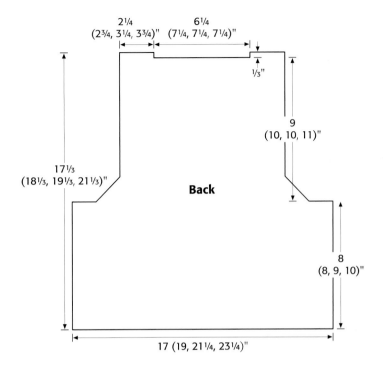

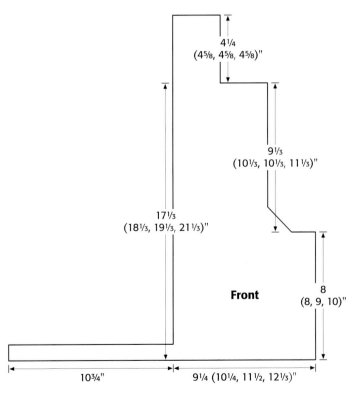

Day to Evening Elegance

A wonderful vest crocheted with simple color changes will add some sparkle

to your office wear or some glamour to your evening. Worn with pants or a skirt

or over just the right dress, this beautiful little vest, with its flattering lines

and narrow waist, will enhance any figure. 🖌

Skill Level: Experienced ◼◼◼▸

Sizes: Small (Medium, Large, X-Large, XX-Large)

Finished Bust: 37⅜ (39, 41⅜, 43, 45⅜)"

Finished Length: 19¼ (19¼, 20¾, 20¾, 22¼)"

MATERIALS

MC 4 (5, 6, 8, 9) skeins of Maratona by Lane Borgosesia from Trendsetter Yarns (100% extra fine merino wool; 50 g [1.75 oz]; 110 yds [100 m]); color 1343 **[4]**

CC 4 (4, 5, 6, 6) skeins of Charming from Trendsetter Yarns (65% polyester, 35% polyamide tactel; 20 g; 120 yds), color 60. *Work with 2 strands throughout.* **[2]**

H-8 (5 mm), I-9 (5.5 mm), and J-10 (6 mm) crochet hooks or size required to obtain gauge

Coilless safety pins

1 button, 1" square

GAUGE

15 sts and 20 rows = 4" in sc with I hook and 1 strand of MC or 2 strands of CC

14 sts and 19 rows = 4" in sc with J hook and 1 strand of MC or 2 strands of CC

Note: The body of the vest starts with the I hook, so it is narrower at the waist. The upper body is enlarged slightly by changing to the J hook and working a looser st gauge. The same gauge must be achieved by using 1 strand of the main color or 2 strands of the contrasting color with the appropriate hook since they are worked at the same time on the fronts.

PATTERN STITCH

All rows: Ch 1, sc in each st across, turn.

Intarsia

The border at the center front is crocheted at the same time as the body of the vest, so the colors need to be interlocked as they are changed by using a technique known as intarsia. To work intarsia:

- Each yarn must be on a separate ball or bobbin.
- Leave the last 2 loops of old color on the hook before starting a new color, yarn over the hook with the new color and draw it through the 2 remaining loops on the hook. Continue by using the new color for as many stitches as required.
- Always drop the color not in use to the back of the work.
- Pull tightly so that there is no gap or hole when a new color is started and an old color is dropped.

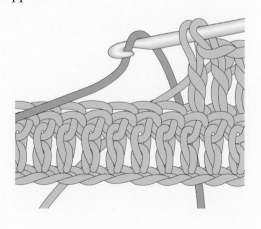

BACK

- With I hook and 1 strand of MC, ch 69 (72, 76, 80, 83), working into loop on WS of ch for all sts, sc in 2nd ch from hook and in each ch across, turn—68 (71, 75, 79, 82) sts.

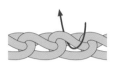

- **(RS):** Mark RS with safety pin. Beg patt st and work until back measures 4 (4, 4½, 5, 5)". Change to J hook, cont in patt until side measures 10 (10, 11, 11, 12)", end with completed WS row.
- **Armholes:** Sl st across next 8 (8, 9, 9, 9) sts, ch 1, sc to last 7 (7, 8, 8, 8) sts, turn. Cont in patt, working sc2tog at beg and end of next 4 (4, 5, 5, 6) rows—46 (49, 49, 53, 54) sts. Cont in patt until armhole measures 5½ (5½, 6, 6, 6½)", end with completed WS row. Change to 2 strands of CC, cont in patt until armhole measures 8½ (8½, 9, 9, 9½)", end with completed WS row.
- **Right shoulder:** Ch 1, work across first 12 (13, 13, 14, 14) sts, turn. **Ch 1, sc2tog, sc to last 4 (4, 4, 5, 5) sts, *sl st in next st, turn, sl st in next st, sc to end*, turn. Ch 1, sc in next 3 (4, 4, 4, 4) sts, rep from * to *. Fasten off.**
- **Left shoulder:** With RS facing, reattach yarn 12 (13, 13, 14, 14) sts from end, work from ** to ** above—22 (23, 23, 25, 26) sts rem unworked in center for back neck.

LEFT FRONT

- With I hook and 1 strand of MC, ch 34 (35, 38, 39, 41), drop MC, join 2 strands of CC and ch 12 (13, 13, 14, 14). Working into loop on WS of ch for all sts, sc in 2nd ch from hook and in each ch across, turn—45 (47, 50, 52, 54) sts; change colors as necessary per intarsia directions in box on facing page.

- **RS:** Mark RS with safety pin. Beg patt st, AT SAME TIME sc2tog on MC side of front edge every 3 (3, 3, 3, 3) rows until 1 MC st rem, work last sc2tog with last MC st and first CC st. Last dec will occur after armhole shaping is completed.

- WHILE YOU CONT DEC, when front measures 4 (4, 4½, 5, 5)" from beg, change to size J hook, cont in patt until side measures 10 (10, 11, 11, 12)", end with completed WS row.

- WHILE YOU CONT DEC, shape armhole: Sl st across next 8 (8, 9, 9, 9) sts, ch 1, work to end of row, turn. Cont in patt, working sc2tog at armhole edge on next 4 (4, 5, 5, 6) rows. Cont in patt until armhole measures 8½ (8½, 9, 9, 9½)", end with completed RS row, turn—11 (12, 12, 13, 13) sts.

- **Shape shoulder:** Ch 1, sc to last 4 (4, 4, 5, 5) sts, *sl st in next st, turn, sl st in next st, sc to end*, turn. Ch 1, sc in next 3 (4, 4, 4, 4) sts, rep from * to *. Fasten off.

RIGHT FRONT

- With I hook and CC, ch 11 (12, 12, 13, 13), join MC and ch 35 (36, 39, 40, 42). Working into loop on WS of ch for all sts, sc in 2nd ch from hook and in each ch across, turn—45 (47, 50, 52, 54) sts. Change colors as necessary per intarsia directions on facing page.

- **RS:** Mark RS with safety pin. Beg patt st, AT SAME TIME sc2tog on MC side of front edge every 3 (3, 3, 3, 3) rows until 1 MC st rem, working last sc2tog with last MC st and first CC st—11 (12, 12, 13, 13) sts in CC. Last dec will occur after armhole shaping.

- WHILE YOU CONT DEC, work buttonhole when front measures 1½" from beg. With RS facing, work 4 sc in CC, ch 3, sk 3 sts, cont across row. **Next row:** Work row as established, working 3 sc in ch-3 sp of buttonhole. If your button is larger or smaller, adjust the number of chs and the number of sts you sk to fit the button, but do not change the number of sts before the buttonhole.

- WHILE YOU CONT DEC, when front measures 4 (4, 4½, 5, 5)", change to J hook, cont in patt until side measures 10 (10, 11, 11, 12)", end with completed WS row.

- WHILE YOU CONT DEC, shape armhole: Ch 1, work to last 7 (7, 8, 8, 8) sts, turn. Cont in patt, sc2tog at armhole edge on next 4 (4, 5, 5, 6) rows. Cont in patt until armhole measures 8½ (8½, 9, 9, 9½)", end with completed WS row, turn—11 (12, 12, 13, 13) sts.

- **Shape shoulder:** Ch 1, sc to last 4 (4, 4, 5, 5) sts, *sl st in next st, turn, sl st in next st, sc to end*, turn. Ch 1, sc in next 3 (4, 4, 4, 4) sts, rep from * to *. Fasten off.

FINISHING

- Weave shoulder seams and side seams tog.

- **Front bands and neckband:** With RS facing, H hook, 2 strands of CC, and starting at right front bottom edge of CC section next to MC, sc in each st across bottom edge, 2 sc in corner, 3 sc for every 4 rows to back neck, skipping 4 sts evenly spaced across back neck, sc down left front to match number of sc worked on right front, 2 sc in corner, 1 sc in each st across lower edge to end of CC section. Fasten off.

- **Armbands:** With RS facing, H hook, MC, and starting at beg of MC section, 1 sc in 2 out of every 3 rows in MC section only. Fasten off. Rep for CC section by using 2 strands of CC. Fasten off. Rep for 2nd armband.

- Gently mist with water. Lay flat to dry. There should be very little blocking required. Gently steam, if necessary, to keep points at center front flat.

- Sew on button.

- Reinforce buttonhole with single strand of CC and buttonhole stitch.

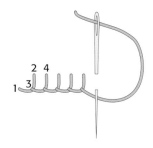

Buttonhole Stitch

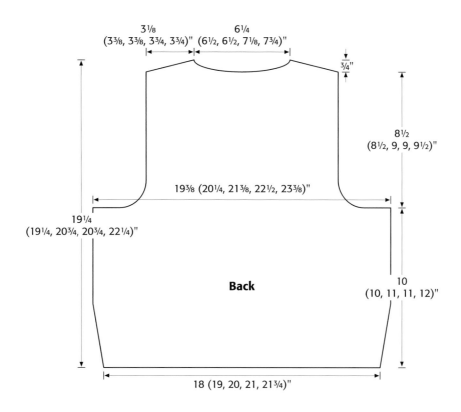

3⅛
(3⅜, 3⅜, 3¾, 3¾)" 6¼
(6½, 6½, 7⅛, 7¾)"

¾"

8½
(8½, 9, 9, 9½)"

19⅜ (20¼, 21⅜, 22½, 23⅜)"

19¼
(19¼, 20¾, 20¾, 22¼)"

Back

10
(10, 11, 11, 12)"

18 (19, 20, 21, 21¾)"

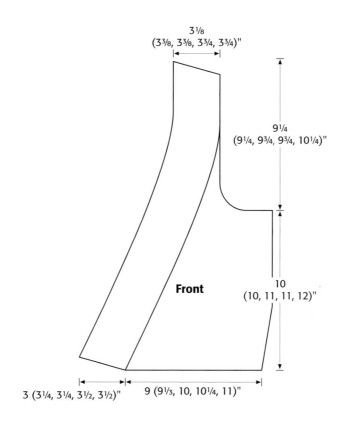

3⅛
(3⅜, 3⅜, 3¾, 3¾)"

9¼
(9¼, 9¾, 9¾, 10¼)"

Front

10
(10, 11, 11, 12)"

3 (3¼, 3¼, 3½, 3½)" 9 (9⅓, 10, 10¼, 11)"

Fall Apples

This lightweight wool-blend yarn is perfect for most seasons.

The ribbed bands make it fit like a knitted vest. The design is simple, but the effect

of the tweed yarn combined with the pattern stitch is fabulous. 🔥

Skill Level: Intermediate ■■■▢

Sizes: X-Small (Small, Medium, Large, X-Large)

Finished Bust: 33 (36, 40½, 45, 49)"

Finished Length: 20½ (21 ¾, 22½, 23½, 24½)"

MATERIALS

5 (5, 6, 7, 8) skeins of Sisik from Dale of Norway (30% wool, 30% mohair, 34% acrylic, 6% rayon; 50 g [1.75 oz]; 150 yds [135 m]); color 167 🟤③

F-5 (3.75 mm) crochet hook or size required to obtain gauge

Coilless safety pins

GAUGE

15 hdc and 12 rows = 4" in patt st

PATTERN STITCH

Multiple of 2 sts

All rows: Ch 2 (count as hdc), sk 1 st, (2 hdc in next st, sk 1 st) across, end with 2 hdc in tch, turn.

completed WS row.

- **Armholes:** Sl st across next 7 (7, 9, 9, 9) sts, ch 2 (count as hdc), work in patt to last 6 (6, 8, 8, 8) sts, turn. Cont in patt, working dec at beg and end of next 4 (4, 4, 4, 5) rows—42 (48, 52, 64, 66) sts. Cont in patt until armhole measures 8 (8¾, 9, 9½, 10)", end with completed WS row.

- **Right shoulder:** Work in patt for 8 (11, 12, 16, 18) sts, turn. Work 1 more row in patt. Fasten off.

- **Left shoulder:** With RS facing, attach yarn in st 9 (12, 13, 17, 19) from end of row, ch 2 (count as hdc), cont in patt to end of row, turn. Work 1 more row in patt, fasten off—24 (24, 26, 26, 28) sts rem unworked for back neck.

FRONT

- Work as for back until piece measures 12 (12½, 13, 13½, 14)" from beg, end with completed WS row.

- **Armhole:** Sl st across next 7 (7, 9, 9, 9) sts, ch 2 (count as hdc), work in patt to last 6 (6, 8, 8, 8) sts, turn. **Next row:** cont in patt, work dec at beg and end as for back.

- **Right shoulder:** On next RS row, divide for V-neck. Insert safety pin in st 25 (28, 30, 34, 38) and out of st 26 (29, 31, 35, 39). These 2 sts will not be worked; they are point of V-neck. Working each side separately, dec at neck before 2 sts marked with pin. Work a neck dec every row and AT SAME TIME cont with armhole dec as given for back until there are 9 (12, 13, 17, 19) sts. When armhole measures same as back, fasten off.

- **Left shoulder:** With RS facing, reattach yarn in st to left of sts with pin at center front. Work as for right shoulder, reversing shaping.

BACK

Dec at beg of row: Ch 2, (count as hdc), sk 2 sts, cont in patt.

Dec at end of row: Work to last 2 sts, sk these 2 sts, 1 hdc in tch, turn.

- **Bottom border (RS):** Ch 9 (9, 9, 10, 11), sc in 2nd ch from hook and in each ch across, mark this side as RS with safety pin, turn. Ch 1, sc in blo across, turn. Rep this row for a total of 62 (68, 76, 84, 92) rows, end with completed WS row, turn so that long side of border faces up.

- Ch 1, sc in each row across top of border, mark this side as RS with safety pin, turn—62 (68, 76, 84, 92) sts.

- Beg patt st and work until piece measures 12 (12½, 13, 13½, 14)" from beg, end with

FINISHING

- Sl st shoulder seams tog.

- Weave side seams tog.

- **Armbands:** Ch 6 (6, 6, 7, 8) sts, work as for bottom border until armband fits around armhole slightly stretched. Weave ends of armband sts tog. Place the seam of the armband next to underarm seam and pin long edge of band to edge of armhole with safety pins, marking halfway and quarter points. Whipstitch band to edge, gently stretching band as you work. The band should butt up next to the edge; there should be no seam allowance since the 2 edges are sitting next to each other. Rep for 2nd armband.

- **Neckband:** Work as for armhole band until it fits around neck opening slightly stretched. Do not weave ends of neckband tog. Pin band to neck edge as for armholes, starting at center front. Ends of band will overlap at center front. Whipstitch band to neck edge as for armbands. When completed, lap right band over left band and whipstitch to edge of V-neck on RS at center front. Whipstitch left band to edge of V-neck on WS at center front.

- Mist with water and lay flat to dry.

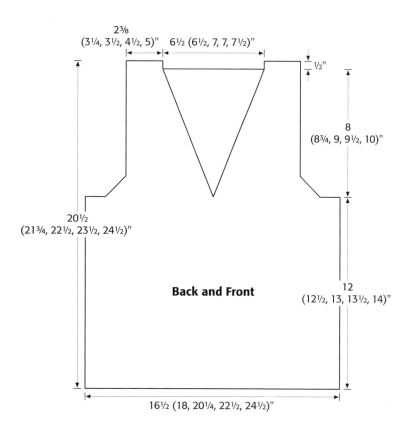

2⅜ (3¼, 3½, 4½, 5)"   6½ (6½, 7, 7, 7½)"   ½"

8 (8¾, 9, 9½, 10)"

20½ (21¾, 22½, 23½, 24½)"

Back and Front

12 (12½, 13, 13½, 14)"

16½ (18, 20¼, 22½, 24½)"

Burnt Embers

The colors in this yarn are reminiscent of a burning fire and the glowing embers after the fire has died down. The rich texture, pattern, and warm colors make this the perfect vest for a walk in the park or a casual day at work. 🔥

Skill Level: Easy ◀■□▷

Sizes: Small (Medium, Large, X-Large)

Finished Bust: 36 (40, 44, 48)"

Finished Length: 21 (22½, 24, 25½)"

MATERIALS

7 (8, 9, 11) skeins of Odyssey by Reynolds Yarns (100% wool; 50 g; 104 yds); color 442 **③**

G-6 (4 mm), H-8 (5 mm), and I-9 (5.5 mm) crochet hooks or size required to obtain gauge

Coilless safety pin

GAUGE

12 sts and 14 rows = 4" in patt st with size H hook

PATTERN STITCH

All rows: Ch 2 (count as hdc), hdc in sp between 2 hdc of previous row across. (First row is RS row.)

BACK

- With size J hook, ch 55 (61, 67, 73), sc in 2nd ch from hook and in each ch across, turn—54 (60, 66, 72) sts. Change to size H hook, ch 2 (count as hdc), hdc in each st across. Beg patt st and work until side measures 12 (13, 14, 15)", end with completed WS row.*

- **Armhole shaping:** Sl st across 7 (8, 8, 9) sts, ch 2 (count as hdc), work in patt to last 6 (7, 7, 8) sts, turn—42 (46, 52, 56) sts. Cont in patt, dec 1 st at each end by skipping 1 sp between 2 hdc every row 3 (3, 4, 4) times—36 (40, 44, 48) sts.

- Cont in patt until armhole measures 8 (8½, 9, 9½)", end with completed WS row.

- **Right shoulder:** Ch 2 (count as hdc), work across next 8 (9, 11, 11) spaces, turn. Cont in patt, dec 1 st at neck edge as for armhole every row 2 times—7 (8, 10, 10) sts. When armhole measures 9 (9½, 10, 10½)", fasten off.

- **Left shoulder:** With RS facing, reattach yarn in sp 9 (10, 12, 12) from end of row, ch 2 (count as hdc), work in patt to end. Cont in patt, dec 1 st at neck edge as for armhole every row 2 times—7 (8, 10, 10) sts. When armhole measures 9 (9½, 10, 10½)", fasten off—18 (20, 20, 24) sts rem unworked for back neck.

FRONT

- Work as for back to *.

- Mark center front by inserting safety pin into sp 26 (29, 32, 35) and out of sp 27 (30, 33, 36).

- **Left front:** Sl st across 7 (8, 8, 9) sts, ch 2 (count as hdc), work to center including sp 26 (29, 32, 35), where safety pin is going in, turn. Cont armhole shaping as for back and AT SAME TIME at neck edge dec 1 st by skipping 1 sp between 2 hdc every RS row 10 (11, 11, 13) times—7 (8, 10, 10) sts. Cont until armhole measures same as back. Fasten off.

- **Right front:** With RS facing, reattach yarn in sp 27 (30, 33, 36) where safety pin is coming out, work in patt to last 6 (7, 7, 8) sts, turn. Ch 2 (count as hdc), cont armhole shaping as for back and AT SAME TIME at neck edge dec 1 st as above, every RS row 10 (11, 11, 13) times—7 (8, 10, 10) sts. Cont until armhole measures same as back. Fasten off.

FINISHING

- Whipstitch shoulder seams tog.
- Weave side seams tog.
- **Neckband:** With RS facing, size G hook, and starting at right shoulder seam, sc 4 (4, 4, 4) sts to back neck, sc 18 (20, 20, 24) sts across back neck, sc 4 (4, 4, 4) sts to shoulder seam, sc 30 (32, 34, 36) sts to center front, sc in each sp where pin was located, sc 30 (32, 34, 36) sts to right shoulder seam. Join with a sl st—88 (94, 98, 106) sts. Mark center front with safety pin. **Next 2 rows:** Ch 1, sc in each st to 2 sts before center front, sc2tog twice, sc to end, join with sl st. Fasten off.

- **Armbands:** With RS facing, size G hook, and starting at underarm seam, sc in each st across first half of underarm sts, sc in each row around to opposite side, sc in each rem underarm st. Join with sl st. Ch 1, sc in each st around, working a sc2tog at shoulder seam, join with sl st. Ch 1, sc in each st around, join with a sl st. Fasten off. Rep for 2nd armband.

- Mist with water and lay flat to dry. Rep for other side.

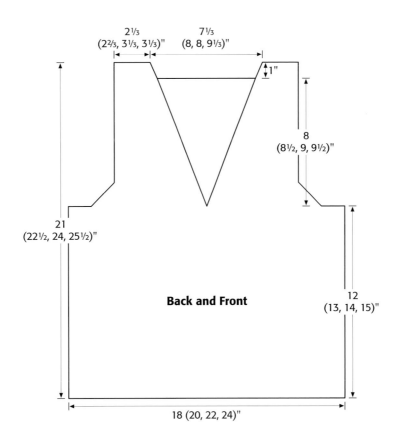

2⅓
(2⅔, 3⅓, 3⅓)"

7⅓
(8, 8, 9⅓)"

1"

8
(8½, 9, 9½)"

21
(22½, 24, 25½)"

Back and Front

12
(13, 14, 15)"

18 (20, 22, 24)"

Waikiki

The name and the yarn make me think of summer and great vacations at the beach.

This vest would be wonderful over a bathing suit or dressed up to go out to dinner.

The drape of the rayon and cotton make this vest easy to wear and easy to pack.

So how about a trip to Hawaii, where you can wear your vest on the beaches

of Waikiki? If you can't make it to Hawaii, how about just wearing it to the

grocery store? It will make you feel like you're on vacation.

Skill Level: Intermediate ■■■□

Sizes: Small (Medium, Large, X-Large, XX-Large)

Finished Bust: 34 (39, 42, 46, 50)"

Finished Length: 23 (23, 24½, 26, 26½)"

MATERIALS

8 (8, 10, 12, 14) skeins of Waikiki by Crystal Palace (65% rayon, 35% cotton; 50 g; 100 yds); color 2889

D-3 (3.25 mm), F-5 (3.75 mm), and G-6 (4 mm) crochet hooks or size required to obtain gauge

4 buttons, ¾" diameter

Coilless safety pin

GAUGE

20 sts and 20 rows = 4" in body patt st with size G hook

PATTERN STITCHES

Openwork Border

Multiple of 2 plus 1

Foundation row (RS): Ch 3 (count as ch 1 and 1 dc), *sk 1 st, dc in next st, ch 1, rep from * to last 2 sts, sk 1 st, dc in last st, turn.

Row 1: Ch 2, (count as dc), *dc in next ch-1 sp, ch 1, rep from * to last ch-1 sp, dc in ch-1 sp, dc in tch, turn.

Row 2: Ch 3 (count as ch 1 and 1 dc), **dc in next ch-1 sp, ch 1, rep from ** to end, dc in tch, turn.

Rep rows 1 and 2.

Body Pattern Stitch

Multiple of 2 plus 1

Foundation row (RS): Ch 1, sc in first st, *sc in next ch-1 sp, ch 1, rep from * to last st, sc in last ch-1 sp, sc in tch, turn.

Row 1: Ch 1, sc in first st, *ch 1, sc in next ch-1 sp, rep from * to last st, sc in last st, turn.

Rep row 1.

BACK

- With size F hook, ch 86 (96, 106, 116, 126), *sc in 2nd ch from hook and in each ch across, turn—85 (95, 105, 115, 125) sts. Ch 1, sc in each st across, turn. Change to size G hook, and work foundation row of openwork border patt. Work rows 1 and 2 of openwork border patt until piece measures 6 (6, 7, 7, 8)", end with completed WS row.

- Work foundation row of body patt. Work row 1 of body patt until side measures 14 (14, 15, 16, 16)", end with completed WS row.*

- **Armhole shaping:** Sl st across 9 (9, 11, 11, 11) sts, ch 1, cont in patt to last 8 (8, 10, 10, 10) sts, turn. Cont in body patt, working sc2tog at beg and end of next 4 (4, 6, 6, 8) rows—61 (71, 73, 83, 89) sts. Cont in body patt until armhole measures 8¼ (8¼, 8¾, 9¼, 9¾)", end with completed WS row.

- **Right shoulder:** Work in body patt across first 13 (15, 15, 17, 19) sts, turn. Cont in patt until armhole measures 9 (9, 9½, 10, 10½)". Fasten off.

- **Left shoulder:** With RS facing, reattach yarn at st 13 (15, 15, 17, 19) from end of row. Cont in body patt until armhole measures the same as right armhole. Fasten off—35 (41, 43, 49, 51) sts rem unworked in center for back neck.

LEFT FRONT

- With size F hook, ch 44 (50, 54, 58, 64). Work from * to * of back—43 (49, 53, 57, 63) sts.

- **Armhole shaping:** Sl st across 9 (9, 11, 11, 11) sts, ch 1, cont in body patt to end, turn. Cont in body patt, working sc2tog at armhole edge on next 4 (4, 6, 6, 8) rows and AT SAME TIME sc2tog at neck edge EOR 18 (22, 22, 24, 26) times—13 (15, 15, 17, 19) sts. Cont in body patt until armhole measures 9 (9, 9½, 10, 10½)". Fasten off.

RIGHT FRONT

- With size F hook, ch 44 (50, 54, 58, 64). Work from * to * of back—43 (49, 53, 57, 63) sts.

- **Armhole shaping:** Ch 1, work in body patt to last 8 (8, 10, 10, 10) sts, turn. Cont in body patt, working sc2tog at neck edge EOR 18 (22, 22, 24, 26) times and AT SAME TIME sc2tog at armhole edge on next 4, (4, 6, 6, 8) rows—13 (15, 15, 17, 19) sts. Cont in body patt until armhole measures 9 (9, 9½, 10, 10½)". Fasten off.

FINISHING

- Whipstitch shoulder seams and side seams tog. Leave openwork border open at bottom edges of side seams to create a slit. The slubs on the yarn can make the yarn a bit difficult to sew. If you have difficulty with this, strip away the ply where the slubs are to make the sewing easier, or use matching embroidery floss in place of the yarn.

- **Front bands and neckband:** With RS facing, size D hook, and starting at lower right edge, sc 38 (38, 42, 42, 46) sts across edge of openwork border patt, sc 38 (38, 38, 42, 42) sts across edge of body patt, mark V-neck with safety pin, sc 47 (47, 49, 51, 53) sts to right shoulder, sc 3 (3, 3, 3, 3) sts to back neck, sc 35 (41, 43, 49, 51) sts across back neck, sc 3 (3, 3, 3, 3) sts to left shoulder, sc 47 (47, 49, 51, 53) sts to start of V-neck, sc 38 (38, 38, 42, 42) sts across edge of body patt, sc 38 (38, 42, 42, 46) sts across edge of openwork border patt—287 (293, 307, 325, 339) sts. **Next 2 rows:** ch 1, sc in each st around, turn.

- **Buttonhole row (WS):** Ch 1, work to beg of V-neck marked with a safety pin. On right front, work buttonholes as follows: *Ch 2, sk 2 sts, sc in next 10 (10, 11, 11, 11,) sts, rep from * 2 more times, ch 2, sk 2 sts, sc in next st, cont to end of row, turn. Ch 1, work to ch-2 sp of buttonholes, work 2 sc over ch-2 sp, cont to end of row, turn. Ch 1, sc in each st. Fasten off.

- **Armbands:** With RS facing, size D hook, and starting at underarm seam, sc 11 (11, 12, 12, 12) sts across first half of underarm sts, sk 1 st in corner, sc 45 (45, 47, 49, 49) sts to shoulder, sc 45 (45, 47, 49, 49) sts to lower edge of armhole, sk 1 st in corner, sc 11 (11, 12, 12, 12) sts across rem underarm sts—112 (112, 118, 122, 122) sts. Join with a sl st. Ch 1, sc in each st around, sk 1 st in corners, join with sl st. Fasten off. Rep for 2nd armband.

- **Bottom band and side-seam vents:** With RS facing, size D hook, and starting at left lower front edge, sc into each st across lower edge of front to corner, *3 sc in corner, 2 sc in each dc on edge of openwork border patt of vent, 1 sc in seam, 2 sc in each dc on edge of openwork border patt of vent, 3 sc in corner,* 1 sc in each st across bottom of back, rep from * to *, 1 sc in each st to lower right front, turn. Ch 1, sc in each st across, working 3 sc in corners. Fasten off.

- Mist with water and lay flat to dry; lay a heavy towel over vest.

- Sew on buttons.

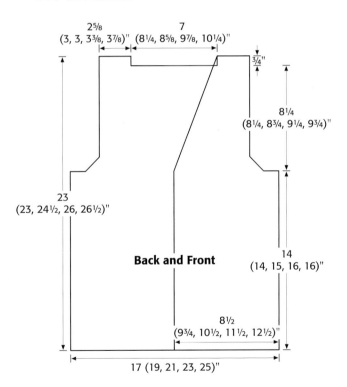

Back and Front

2⁵⁄₈ (3, 3, 3³⁄₈, 3⁷⁄₈)"

7 (8¹⁄₄, 8⁵⁄₈, 9⁷⁄₈, 10¹⁄₄)"

³⁄₄"

8¹⁄₄ (8¹⁄₄, 8³⁄₄, 9¹⁄₄, 9³⁄₄)"

23 (23, 24¹⁄₂, 26, 26¹⁄₂)"

14 (14, 15, 16, 16)"

8¹⁄₂ (9³⁄₄, 10¹⁄₂, 11¹⁄₂, 12¹⁄₂)"

17 (19, 21, 23, 25)"

Denim and Silk

What a fabulous vest to wear with jeans or with rich-colored pants or skirts!

Perfect for all seasons, the silk-and-rayon blend drapes beautifully on the body.

There's lots of texture in the pattern so you get the full feel of the wonderful yarn. 🖋

Skill Level: Intermediate ■■■◻

Sizes: Small (Medium, Large, X-Large, XX-Large)

Finished Bust: 35½ (38¾, 42¼, 45¾, 49)"

Finished Length: 22 (22, 23½, 25, 26)"

MATERIALS

10 (10, 12, 14, 16) skeins of Denim Silk by Berroco (80% rayon, 20% silk; 50 g [1.75 oz]; 105 yds [97 m]); color 1413 【4】

G-6 (4 mm) and H-8 (5 mm) crochet hooks or size required to obtain gauge

Coilless safety pins

GAUGE

14 sts and 14 rows = 4" in patt st with size H hook

Note: When this yarn is crocheted, it will feel very stiff and the edges will ruffle until it is wet and blocked. To get the correct gauge, you must wet and block the gauge swatch, too.

PATTERN STITCH

Multiple of 3 plus 2

Foundation row (RS): Ch 2 (count as hdc), hdc in next st, *FPdc around next st 2 rows below, hdc in next 2 sts, rep from * to end, turn.

Row 1: Ch 1, sc in each st across, turn.

Row 2: Ch 2 (count as hdc), hdc in next st, *FPdc around FPdc 2 rows below, hdc in next 2 sts, rep from * to end, turn.

Rep rows 1 and 2 for patt.

BACK

- With size H hook, ch 63 (69, 75, 80, 87) sts, hdc in 3rd ch from hook (count as hdc) and in each ch across, turn—62 (68, 74, 80, 86) sts. Ch 2 (count as hdc), hdc in each st across, turn. Ch 1, sc in each st across, turn.

- Work foundation row. Work rows 1 and 2 of patt st until side measures 12 (12, 13, 14, 15)", end with completed WS row.

- **Armhole shaping:** Sl st in next 10 (10, 12, 12, 12) sts, ch 2 (count as hdc), cont in patt to last 9 (9, 11, 11, 11) sts—44 (50, 52, 58, 64) sts, turn. Cont in patt until armhole measures 7 (7, 7, 7½, 8)", end with completed WS row.

- **Right shoulder:** Work in patt across first 12 (14, 14, 16, 18) sts, turn. Cont in patt and AT SAME TIME sc2tog at neck edge on next 3 sc rows—9 (11, 11, 13, 15) sts. Cont in patt until armhole measures 10 (10, 10½, 11, 11)", end with completed WS row. Fasten off.

- **Left shoulder:** With RS facing, reattach yarn in st 12 (14, 14, 16, 18) from end of row, turn. Cont in patt, work dec at neck edge and finish as for right shoulder—20 (22, 24, 26, 28) sts rem unworked in center for back neck.

FRONT

- Work as for back until armhole measures 5 (5, 5, 5, 5)", end with completed WS row.

- **Left shoulder:** Work in patt across first 13 (15, 15, 17, 19) sts, turn. Cont in patt and AT SAME TIME sc2tog at neck edge on next 4 sc rows—9 (11, 11, 13, 15) sts. Cont in patt until armhole measures 10 (10, 10½, 11, 11)", end with completed WS row. Fasten off.

- **Right shoulder:** With RS facing, reattach yarn in st 13 (15, 15, 17, 19) from end of row, ch 2, cont in patt and AT SAME TIME work dec at neck edge and finish as for left shoulder—18 (20, 22, 24, 26) sts rem unworked in center for front neck.

FINISHING

- Weave shoulder seams tog.

- **Neckband:** With RS facing, size G hook, and starting at right shoulder seam, sc 16 (17, 18, 18, 20) sts to back neck, mark last st as corner with safety pin, sc 20 (22, 24, 26, 28) sts across back neck, mark last st as corner with safety pin, sc 16 (17, 18, 18, 20) sts to left shoulder, sc 19 (19, 21, 23, 23) sts to front neck, mark last st as corner with safety pin, sc 18 (20, 22, 24, 26) sts across front neck, mark last st as corner with safety pin, sc 19 (19, 21, 23, 23) sts to right shoulder seam, join with sl st—108 (114, 124, 132, 140) sts.* **Next rnd:** Ch 1, sc in each st, skipping 1 st at corners, join with sl st—104 (110, 120, 128, 136) sts. **Next rnd:** Ch 1, (FPdc around sc 2 rows below, sc in next st) around, join with sl st. **Last rnd:** Ch 1, work 1 row rsc. Fasten off.*

- **Armbands:** With RS facing, size G hook, and starting at underarm seam, sc 9 (9, 11, 11, 11) sts across first half of underarm sts, mark last st as corner with safety pin, sc 38 (38, 39, 42, 42) sts to shoulder seam, sc 38 (38, 39, 42, 42) sts to underarm sts of armhole, mark last st as corner with safety pin, sc 9 (9, 11, 11, 11) sts in rem underarm sts, join with a sl st—94 (94, 100, 106, 106) sts. Work as for neckband from * to *. Rep for 2nd armband.

- Immerse in water. Gently roll in towel, lay flat to dry, turning frequently. The thickness of the yarn may require a longer drying time. Lay the garment on a dry towel on top of a running dryer to assist with drying. No further blocking is required.

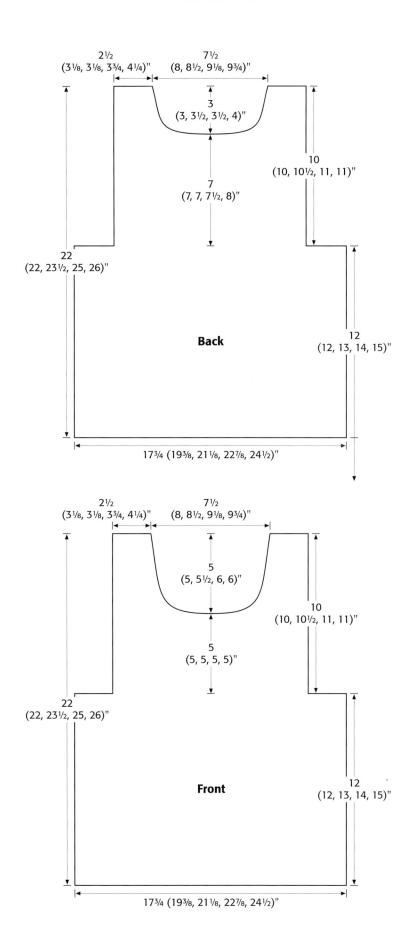

2½
(3⅛, 3⅛, 3¾, 4¼)"

7½
(8, 8½, 9⅛, 9¾)"

3
(3, 3½, 3½, 4)"

10
(10, 10½, 11, 11)"

7
(7, 7, 7½, 8)"

22
(22, 23½, 25, 26)"

Back

12
(12, 13, 14, 15)"

17¾ (19⅜, 21⅛, 22⅞, 24½)"

2½
(3⅛, 3⅛, 3¾, 4¼)"

7½
(8, 8½, 9⅛, 9¾)"

5
(5, 5½, 6, 6)"

10
(10, 10½, 11, 11)"

5
(5, 5, 5, 5)"

22
(22, 23½, 25, 26)"

Front

12
(12, 13, 14, 15)"

17¾ (19⅜, 21⅛, 22⅞, 24½)"

Raspberry Malt

A fabulous, rich cotton and a shell-stitch pattern make a perfect combination that complements the feel and weight of this yarn. There are no buttons or buttonholes so the finishing is simple. This stunning addition to your wardrobe is easy to wear; simply toss it on over a blouse or turtleneck and you're on your way to the office or to run errands.

Skill Level: Intermediate ◼◼◼▢

Sizes: Small (Medium, Large, X-Large)

Finished Bust: 35¾ (42¾, 48¼, 54¼)"

Finished Length: 22 (23½, 24½, 26)"

MATERIALS

4 (5, 5, 6) skeins of King Tut from Knitting Fever (100% cotton; 100 g; 182 yds); color 1972 **③**

E-4 (3.5 mm) crochet hook or size required to obtain gauge

GAUGE

16 dc and 10 rows = 4" in patt st

SHELL PATTERN STITCH

Multiple of 12 plus 1

Foundation row (RS): Ch 2 (count as dc), dc in next 2 dc, *sk 2 dc, 5 dc in next dc, ch 2, sk 4 dc, dc in next 5 dc*, rep from * to *, ending last rep with dc in next 3 dc instead of 5 dc, turn.

Row 1: Ch 2 (count as dc), dc in next 2 dc, *sk ch-2 sp, 5 dc in next dc, ch 2, sk 4 dc, dc in next 5 dc*, rep from * to *, ending last rep with dc in next 3 dc instead of 5 dc, turn.

Rep row 1 for patt.

BACK

- Ch 74 (86, 98, 110), dc in 3rd ch from hook (count as dc) and in each ch across—73 (85, 97, 109) sts, turn. Ch 2 (count as dc), dc in each st across, turn.

- Work foundation row. Work row 1 of patt st until side measures 12 (13, 14, 15)", end with completed WS row.

- **Armhole shaping:** With RS facing, sl st in each of next 13 sts, including ch sts, ch 2 (count as dc), work in patt to last 12 sts, turn—49 (61, 73, 85) sts. Cont in patt until armhole measures 9 (9½, 9½, 10)", end with completed WS row.

- **Right shoulder:** Ch 2 (count as dc), dc in next 9 (11, 16, 19) sts, turn. Ch 2 (count as dc), dc in each st across. Fasten off—10 (12, 17, 20) sts.

- **Left shoulder:** With RS facing, reattach yarn in st 10 (12, 17, 20) from end of row. Ch 2 (count as dc), dc in each st across, turn. Ch 2 (count as dc), dc in each dc across. Fasten off—29 (37, 39, 45) sts rem unworked for back neck.

LEFT FRONT

- ****Ch 36 (44, 49, 55), dc in 3rd ch from hook (count as dc) and in each ch across—35 (43, 48, 54) sts, turn. Ch 2 (count as dc), dc in each st across, turn.****

- **Foundation row (WS):** Ch 2 (count as dc), dc in next 12 (8, 13, 7) dc, work foundation row of shell patt st from * to * 2 (3, 3, 4) times, ending last rep with dc in next 3 dc instead of 5 dc, turn. **Row 1:** Ch 2 (count as dc), dc in next 2 dc, work row 1 of shell patt st from * to * 2 (3, 3, 4) times, ending last rep with dc in next 13 (9, 14, 8) dc instead of 5 dc, turn. **Row 2:** Ch 2 (count as dc), dc in next 12 (8, 13, 7) dc, work row 1 of shell patt st from

* to * 2 (3, 3, 4) times, ending last rep with dc in next 3 dc instead of 5 dc, turn. Rep last 2 rows until side measures 12 (13, 14, 15)", end with completed WS row.

- **Armhole and V-neck shaping:** With RS facing, sl st in each of next 13 (13, 13, 13) sts, including ch sts, turn. Work in patt to last 2 sts, dc2tog at neck edge, turn. Ch 2 (count as dc), cont in patt, working dc2tog at neck edge every row and keeping continuity of patt until 10 (12, 17, 20) sts rem. Cont in patt until armhole is 2 rows shorter than back. **Next 2 rows:** Ch 2 (count as dc), dc in each st across, turn. Fasten off.

RIGHT FRONT

- Work as for left front from ** to **.

- **Foundation row (RS):** Ch 2 (count as dc), dc in next 12 (8, 13, 7) dc, work foundation row of shell patt st from * to * 2 (3, 3, 4) times, ending last rep with dc in next 3 dc instead of 5 dc, turn. **Row 1:** Ch 2 (count as dc), dc in next 2 dc, work row 1 of shell patt st from * to * 2 (3, 3, 4) times, ending last rep with dc in next 13 (9, 14, 8) dc instead of 5 dc, turn. **Row 2:** Ch 2 (count as dc), dc in next 12 (8, 13, 7) dc, work row 1 of shell patt st from * to * 2 (3, 3, 4) times, ending last rep with dc in next 3 dc instead of 5 dc, turn. Rep last 2 rows until side measures 12 (13, 14, 15)", end with completed WS row. There should be same number of rows on both left and right fronts.

- **Armhole and V-neck shaping:** Ch 2 (count as dc), dc2tog, work in patt to last 12 (12, 12, 12) sts, turn. Cont in patt, working dc2tog on every row at neck edge and keeping continuity of patt until 10 (12, 17, 20) sts rem. Cont in patt until armhole is 2 rows shorter than back. **Next 2 rows:** Ch 2 (count as dc), dc in each st across, turn. Fasten off.

FINISHING

- Sl st shoulder seams tog.

- Weave side seams tog.

- **Armbands:** With RS facing, join yarn at underarm seam. Sc in each st across first half of underarm sts, work 2 sc in each dc row around to opposite underarm corner, sc in each rem st of underarm, join with a sl st. Ch 2 (count as dc), dc in each st around, working a dc2tog at each corner of armhole and one at shoulder seam, join with a sl st. Fasten off. Rep for 2nd armband.

- **Neckband:** With RS facing, join yarn at bottom edge of right front, work 2 sc in each dc row to back neck, 1 sc in each dc, and 2 sc in each ch-2 sp to left shoulder, cont down left front, working 2 sc in each dc row to bottom of left front edge, turn. Be sure both fronts have same number of sts. Ch 2 (count as dc), dc in each st around. Ch 1, sc in each st around. Fasten off.

- Lay flat, mist with water, and smooth with hands. Be sure fronts are even and armholes lie flat. Leave flat until dry.

- If you prefer a closure of some sort, this is the perfect vest on which to sew metal clasps.

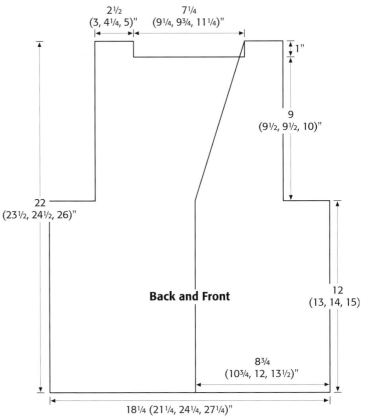

2½ (3, 4¼, 5)"

7¼ (9¼, 9¾, 11¼)"

1"

9 (9½, 9½, 10)"

22 (23½, 24½, 26)"

12 (13, 14, 15)

Back and Front

8¾ (10¾, 12, 13½)"

18¼ (21¼, 24¼, 27¼)"

Spring Camisole

Wear this vest or camisole under a suit to the office or with a fancy skirt to a party.

The beautiful green reminds me of spring, but you can wear it in any season

because the color will go with almost anything. The little lace at the top makes it

fun to wear by itself or under a suit. The yummy, soft yarn doesn't even feel like

wool, but it is. You'll need one of these camisoles in every color available! 🖋

Skill Level: Intermediate ◢■■▢

Sizes: Small (Medium, Large, X-Large, XX-Large)

Finished Bust: 34 (38, 42, 46, 50)"

Finished Length: 20 (21½, 23, 24½, 26)"

MATERIALS

7 (8, 9, 11, 13) skeins of Schoeller Stahl Merino Soft from Skacel Yarns (100% merino Superwash wool; 50 g; 118 yds); color 17 **(3)**

E-4 (3.5 mm), F-5 (3.75 mm), G-6 (4 mm), and H-8 (5 mm) crochet hooks or size required to obtain gauge

GAUGE

20 sts and 24 rows = 4" in body patt st with size H hook

PATTERN STITCHES

Body Pattern Stitch

Worked over even number of sts

Foundation row (RS): Ch 1, sc in first st, *ch 1, sk next sc, sc in next st, rep from * to last st, sc in last st, turn.

Row 1: Ch 1, sc in first st, *ch 1, sc in next ch-1 sp, rep from * to last st, sc in last sc, turn.

Rep row 1 for patt.

Lace Pattern Stitch

Foundation row (RS): Ch 3 (counts as dc and ch 1), *dc in next ch-1 sp, ch 1, rep from * to last ch-1 sp, dc in last ch-1 sp, dc in last st.

Row 1: Ch 3 (counts as dc and ch 1), *dc in next ch-1 sp, ch 1, rep from * to last ch-1 sp, dc in last ch-1 sp (3rd ch in ch 3 of previous row), dc in top of turning ch (2nd ch in ch 3 of previous row).

Rep row 1 for patt.

BACK

- *With size G hook, ch 87 (97, 107, 117, 127), sc in 2nd ch from hook and in each ch across, turn—86 (96, 106, 116, 126) sts.

- Change to size H hook and work body patt foundation row. Work row 1 of body patt until side measures 11 (12, 13, 13½, 14)", end with completed WS row.

- **Armhole shaping:** Sl st across first 11 (13, 13, 15, 17) sts, including ch-1 sps, ch 1, cont in patt to last 10 (12, 12, 14, 16) sts, turn. Cont in patt, working sc2tog at beg and end of next 3 (4, 5, 5, 6) rows—60 (64, 72, 78, 82) sts. Cont in patt until armhole measures 2½ (2½, 3, 3, 3)", end with completed WS row.*

- Work lace patt foundation row. Work row 1 of lace patt until armhole measures 8 (8½, 9, 10, 11)", end with completed WS row.

- **Right shoulder:** Work in lace patt across first 9 (9, 12, 13, 14) sts, dc2tog at neck edge once, turn. Cont in lace patt until armhole measures 9 (9½, 10, 11, 12)". Fasten off—10 (10, 13, 14, 15) sts.

- **Left shoulder:** With RS facing, reattach yarn in st 11 (11, 14, 15, 16) from end of row, ch 2 (count as dc), dc2tog, cont in lace patt to end of row, turn. Cont in lace patt until armhole measures 9 (9½, 10, 11, 12)". Fasten off—38 (42, 44, 48, 50) sts rem unworked in center for back neck.

FRONT

- Work as for back from * to *. Work lace patt foundation row. Work row 1 of lace patt until lace section measures 1½ (2, 2, 2, 2)", end with completed WS row.

- **Left shoulder:** Work in lace patt across first 11 (12, 15, 17, 18) sts, turn. Cont in lace patt, working dc2tog at neck edge 3 (4, 4, 5, 5) times—10 (10, 13, 14, 15) sts. Cont in lace patt until armhole measures 9 (9½, 10, 11, 12)". Fasten off.

Right shoulder: With RS facing, reattach yarn in st 13 (14, 17, 19, 20) from end of row, ch 2 (count as dc), dc2tog, cont in lace patt to end of row. Cont in lace patt, working dc2tog at neck edge 2 (3, 3, 4, 4) more times—10 (10, 13, 14, 15) sts. Cont in lace patt until armhole measures 9 (9½, 10, 11, 12)". Fasten off—34 (36, 38, 40, 42) sts rem unworked in center for front neck.

FINISHING

- Whipstitch shoulder seams tog.
- Weave side seams tog.
- **Neckband:** With RS facing, size F hook, and starting at right shoulder seam, sc 4 (4, 4, 4, 4) sts to back neck, sc 38 (42, 44, 48, 50) sts across back neck, sc 4 (4, 4, 4, 4) sts to left shoulder seam, sc 2 (2, 2, 2, 2) sts in each dc to front neck, sc 34 (36, 38, 40, 42) sts across front neck, sc 2 (2, 2, 2, 2) sts in each dc to right shoulder, join with a sl st. Change to size E hook, ch 1, sc in each st, join with sl st. Ch 1, work 1 row rsc. Fasten off.

- **Armbands:** With RS facing, size F hook, and starting at underarm seam, work 1 sc in first half of underarm sts, 1 sc in each sc row, 2 sc in each dc row around, 1 sc in rem sts of underarm, join with sl st. Change to size E hook, ch 1, sc in each st around, join with sl st. Ch 1, work 1 row rsc. Fasten off. Rep for 2nd armband.

- Mist with water and lay flat to dry. Concentrate the water on the neckband and armbands, shaping and pinning as necessary. You may need to rep for other side. Do not remove until completely dry.

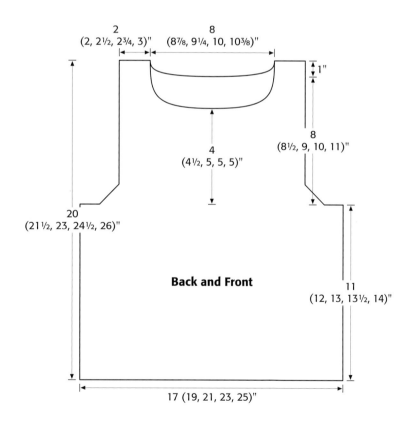

2
(2, 2½, 2¾, 3)"

8
(8⅞, 9¼, 10, 10⅜)"

1"

4
(4½, 5, 5, 5)"

8
(8½, 9, 10, 11)"

20
(21½, 23, 24½, 26)"

Back and Front

11
(12, 13, 13½, 14)"

17 (19, 21, 23, 25)"

The Great Outdoors

Make this great outdoor vest for you, or make a larger size for the man in your life.

The bulky-weight yarn makes this a simple and quick project.

The zipper adds a fabulous detail to make this vest great for a day

of working outdoors or hanging around the house.

Skill Level: Easy ◼◼☐◻

Sizes: Small (Medium, Large, X-Large, XX-Large)

Finished Bust: 36 (42, 44, 48, 52)"

Finished Length: 24 (25, 26, 26½, 28)"

MATERIALS

8 (9, 10, 11, 13) skeins of Excellent by Schoeller Stahl from Skacel Yarns (67% wool, 28% acrylic, 5% alpaca; 50 g; 50 m); color 811 🔟

K-10½ (6.5 mm) and L-11 (8 mm) crochet hooks or size required to obtain gauge

16" to 18" plastic separating jacket zipper*

Small amount of contrasting crochet thread or fine cotton yarn

*If you can't find a zipper of the correct length in the correct color, you can trim a too-long zipper to fit (see page 61).

GAUGE

8 sts and 9 rows = 4" in patt st with size L hook

PATTERN STITCH

The patt st alternates a row of hdc with a row of sc. The ch 1 at the beg of the rows is made regardless of whether the row is hdc or sc and does not count as a st. This is done because if a hdc is worked at the beg of the hdc rows and a sc worked at the beg on the sc rows, as it normally would be worked, the piece will have one edge longer than the other and it will not hang straight.

Row 1 (RS): Ch 1, sc in each st across, turn.

Row 2: Ch 1, hdc in each st across, turn.

Rep rows 1 and 2 for patt.

BACK

- With size K hook, ch 37 (41, 45, 49, 53) sts, sc in 2nd ch from hook and in each ch across—36 (40, 44, 48, 52) sts. **Next 2 rows:** Ch 1, sc in each st across, turn.

- **Next row (RS):** Change to size L hook, beg patt st, and work until side measures 14 (14, 15, 15, 16)", end with completed WS row.

- **Armhole shaping:** Sl st across next 7 (9, 9, 11, 11) sts, ch 1, cont in patt to last 6 (8, 8, 10, 10) sts, turn—24 (24, 28, 28, 32) sts. Cont in patt until armhole measures 8 (9, 9, 9½, 10)", end with completed WS row.

- **Right shoulder:** Work in patt across 5 (5, 6, 6, 7) sts for 2", end with hdc row. Fasten off.

- **Left shoulder:** With RS facing, reattach yarn in st 5 (5, 6, 6, 7) from end of row, ch 1, work in patt for 2", end with hdc row. Fasten off—14 (14, 16, 16, 18) sts rem unworked for back neck.

LEFT FRONT

- *With size K hook, ch 19 (21, 23, 25, 27) sts, sc in 2nd ch from hook and in each ch across, turn—18 (20, 22, 24, 26) sts. **Next 2 rows:** Ch 1, sc in each st across, turn.

- Change to size L hook, beg patt st, and work until side measures 14 (14, 15, 15, 16)", end with completed WS row. Be sure front and back have same number of rows.*

- **Armhole and V-neck shaping:** Sl st across next 7 (9, 9, 11, 11) sts, ch 1, cont in patt, working sc2tog at neck edge (even if the row being worked is a hdc row) until 5 (5, 6, 6, 7) sts rem. Cont in patt until armhole measures same as back. Fasten off.

RIGHT FRONT

- Work as for left front from * to *.

- **Armhole and V-neck shaping:** Work in patt to last 6 (8, 8, 10, 10) sts, turn. Cont in patt, working sc2tog at neck edge until 5 (5, 6, 6, 7) sts rem. Cont in patt until armhole measures same as back. Fasten off.

FINISHING

- Sl st shoulder seams tog.

- Weave side seams tog.

- **Armbands:** With size K hook, attach yarn at underarm seam, sc in each st across first half of underarm sts, 2 sc in each hdc row and 1 sc in each sc row around to opposite corner, 1 sc in each rem underarm st, join with a sl st. **Next 4 rows:** Ch 1, sc in each st around, sk 1 st at each armhole corner, join with sl st. Fasten off. Rep for 2nd armband.

- **Neckband:** With RS facing and size K hook, attach yarn at lower right front, work 1 sc in each sc row, 2 sc in each hdc row to back neck, 1 sc in each st across back neck. Cont working 1 sc in each sc row and 2 sc in each hdc row to bottom edge of left front. Be sure both fronts have same number of sts, turn. **Next 3 rows:** Ch 1, sc in each st around, turn. Fasten off.

- **Zipper:** Using crochet thread, whipstitch front of vest closed, matching each st from bottom edge to start of V-neck shaping. Measure zipper against basted edge. If zipper needs to be trimmed, zigzag by sewing machine or overcast by hand about ¼" above where zipper fits into opening. Trim excess zipper about 1" above overcast sts. Trim teeth on excess tape of zipper and tack down extra zipper tape to underside of rem zipper. Baste zipper to wrong side of vest opening. Using matching sewing thread on WS, backstitch zipper in place. Remove basting from front edge and backstitch zipper in place on RS between crochet edge of front and zipper next to teeth. All stitching should be invisible. Remove remaining basting.

• With zipper closed, heavily mist with water and lay flat to dry. Pin edges in several places. Place a heavy towel over vest and allow to dry completely before removing. Rep for other side. The vest will tend to skew around the body unless it is blocked heavily. Steam if necessary.

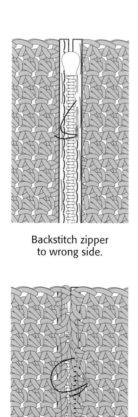

Backstitch zipper
to wrong side.

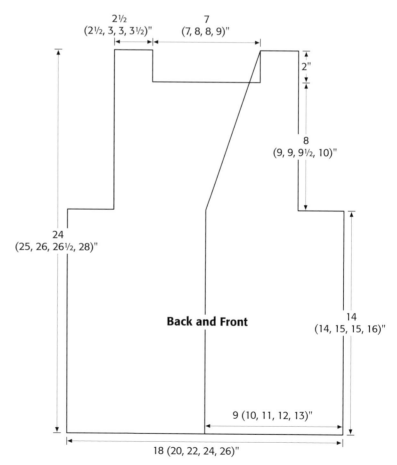

2½
(2½, 3, 3, 3½)"

7
(7, 8, 8, 9)"

2"

8
(9, 9, 9½, 10)"

24
(25, 26, 26½, 28)"

Back and Front

14
(14, 15, 15, 16)"

9 (10, 11, 12, 13)"

18 (20, 22, 24, 26)"

Sideways Stripes

This wonderful yarn makes stripes and creates a pattern all on its own. The color is
perfect for fall and a trip to peep at the leaves or just to the grocery store.
The appeal of crocheting a vest in one piece makes this an engaging project as you
work your way around the body. You won't be able to put this one down
as you watch the colors move up, down, and across the vest.

Skill Level: Experienced ◀◼◼◼
Sizes: Small (Medium, Large, X-Large)
Finished Bust: 36 (40, 44, 48)"
Finished Length: 25¼ (25¼, 26, 26)"

MATERIALS
7 (8, 10, 11) skeins of Silk Garden by Noro (45% silk, 45% kid mohair, 10%
   lamb's wool; 50 g; 100 m); color 34 🄴
H-8 (5 mm) and I-9 (5.5 mm) crochet hooks or size required to obtain gauge
Coilless safety pins
6 buttons, ¾" diameter

GAUGE
12½ sts and 12 rows = 4" in patt st with size I hook

Working with Noro Yarns: All the skeins of same color yarn contain the same
sequence of colors, but each skein may start that sequence in a different place.
When you need to start a new skein of yarn, you'll have to start with the next
color in the sequence to keep the stripes in the correct order, which means you
may have to roll part of the skein into a ball to find the correct color to start with.
The yarn you rolled into a ball will then be used at the end of the skein to
complete the color sequence for that skein of yarn. Because the yarns are always
wound in the same direction, always use the yarn from the skeins in the same
direction, either from the outside or from the inside.

PATTERN STITCH

Row 1 (WS): Ch 2 (count as hdc), hdc in each st across, turn.

Row 2: Ch 1 (do not count as st), sc in blo of each st across, turn. (For smoother edges, sc in both loops of first and last st of row.)

Rep rows 1 and 2 for patt.

LEFT FRONT

Vest is worked in one piece, starting at the left front, working across the back, and ending at the right front.

- With size I hook, ch 68 (68, 68, 68) loosely, sc in 2nd ch from hook and in each ch across, turn—67 (67, 67, 67) sts. Beg patt st. Mark RS with a safety pin. With RS facing, neck edge will be at left.

- When work measures 3 (3½, 3¾, 4)", work 2 hdc or 2 sc into first st at neck edge every row 4 times, depending on what row you're on—71 (71, 71, 71) sts.

- **Neck Shaping:** At end of next RS row, ch 9 (9, 11, 11), turn, hdc in 3rd ch from hook (count as hdc) and in each ch across, cont in patt across row—79 (79, 81, 81) sts.

- ***Shoulder Shaping:** On next 4 WS rows, work hdc2tog at shoulder edge. Mark each row where dec was made with a safety pin. Cont in patt until shoulder measures 3½ (3½, 4, 4½)", end with completed WS row—75 (75, 77, 77) sts.

- **Armhole Shaping:** Work in patt across 47 (47, 47, 47) sts, turn—28 (28, 30, 30) sts rem unworked for armhole. Cont in patt, working hdc2tog at armhole edge on next 2 WS rows—45 (45, 45, 45) sts. Cont in patt until underarm section measures 2 (3, 3½, 4)" from start of armhole shaping. Inc on next 2 WS rows by working 2 hdc into first sc at armhole edge—47 (47, 47, 47) sts. At end of next RS row, ch 29 (29, 31, 31), turn, hdc in 3rd ch from hook (count as hdc) and in each ch across, cont in patt across row—75 (75, 77, 77) sts.*

BACK

- **Shoulder shaping:** Cont in patt, working 2 hdc in first st at shoulder edge on WS rows to coincide with dec rows on front shoulder marked with safety pins. Mark inc with safety pins. Cont in patt until shoulder measures 3½ (3½, 4, 4½)", end with completed WS row—79 (79, 81, 81) sts.

- **Neck shaping:** Work to 3 (3, 4, 4) sts from end of row (neck edge), turn—76 (76, 77, 77) sts. Cont in patt until back neck measures 8 (9, 9½, 10)", end with completed WS row. Work in patt across next RS row, ch 4 (4, 5, 5) at end of row, turn, hdc in 3rd ch from hook (count as hdc) and in each ch across, cont in patt across row—79 (79, 81, 81) sts.

- **Shoulder and armhole shaping:** Work from * to * as for left front.

RIGHT FRONT

- **Shoulder shaping:** Cont in patt, working 2 hdc on hdc rows at shoulder edge on WS to coincide with dec rows on right back shoulder marked with safety pins. Cont in patt until shoulder measures 3½ (3½, 4, 4½)", end with completed WS row—79 (79, 81, 81) sts.

- **Neck Shaping:** On next RS row, work to last 8 (8, 10, 10) sts, turn. Cont in patt, working hdc2tog or sc2tog at neck edge on next 4 rows, depending on what row you're on—67 (67, 67, 67) sts. Mark dec with safety pins.

- Cont until front neck measures 3 (3½, 3¾, 4)" from start of neck shaping, end with completed WS row. Do not fasten off. Place last loop on safety pin.

FINISHING

- With WS facing up, weave shoulder seams tog. Use safety pins to indicate inc and dec at shoulders as a reference to help match shoulders.

- **Front bands and neckband:** With RS facing, place last loop on size H hook, ch 1, sc 64 (64, 64, 64) sts up right front, 3 sc in last st at neck edge, sc 13 (14, 15, 16) sts across front neck edge to inside corner of neck, sk 2 sts, sc 9 (10, 11, 12) sts to back neck, sc 30 (32, 33, 34) sts across back neck, sc 9 (10, 11, 12) sts to inside corner of front neck, sk 2 sts, sc 13 (14, 15, 16) sts across front neck, sc 3 in corner of left front, sc 64 (64, 64, 64) sts down left front edge, turn—208 (214, 219, 224) sc. Ch 1, sc in each st up left front, around front and back neck, working 3 sc in center st at front corners and skipping 2 sts on inside corners of front neck, cont down right front, turn.

- **Buttonhole row (for all sizes):** Ch 1, sc in next 12 sts, (ch 2, sk 2 sts, sc in next 8 sts) 5 times, ch 2, sk 2 sts, cont sc around neck edges, working 3 sc in center st at front corners and sk 2 sts on inside corners of front neck, cont to lower left front, 3 sc in corner of lower left front, sc across entire bottom edge, 3 sc in corner of lower right front, do not turn. Ch 1, sc in each st up right front, working 2 sc in ch-2 sp for each buttonhole, cont around front and back neck, do not sk sts at inside corners of front neck but do work the 3 sts in center st of front corners, cont down left front to bottom edge. Fasten off.

- **Armbands:** With RS facing, H hook, and starting in center of underarm, work 1 sc for each row across lower edge of armhole and 1 sc for each st around armhole, finishing with 1 sc for each row across rem sts of underarm, join with sl st. Ch 1, sc in each st around, join with sl st. Fasten off. Rep for 2nd armband.

- Lay flat, mist with water, pin to shape, and cover with a heavy towel until completely dry. Rep for other side.

- Sew on buttons.

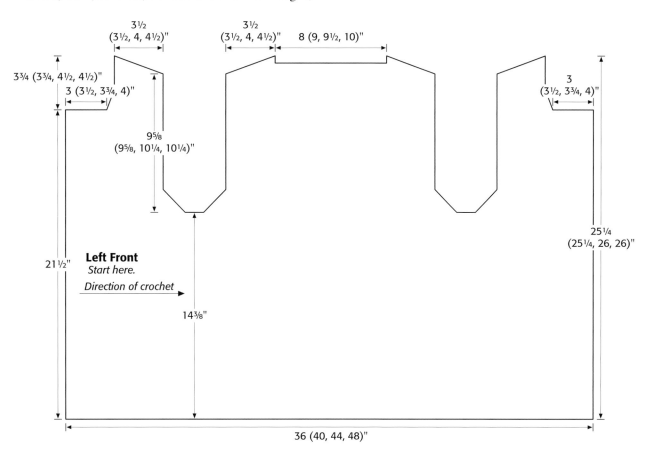

Basket Weave

This boxy pullover vest will look great with jeans for a weekend away as well as with dressy slacks or a skirt for the office. The alpaca in this yarn will keep you warm and cozy no matter where you choose to wear it. I can see it made in any color to show off the wonderful pattern. 🖋

Skill Level: Easy ◼◼☐☐

Sizes: Small (Medium, Large, X-Large)

Finished Bust: 36 (40, 44, 48)"

Finished Length: 23 (24, 25½, 26½)"

MATERIALS

7 (8, 10, 12) skeins of Lana d' Oro by Cascade Yarns (50% superfine alpaca, 50% wool; 50 g [1.75 oz]; 110 yds); color 250 (4)

G-6 (4 mm), I-9 (5.5 mm), and J-10 (6 mm) crochet hooks or size required to obtain gauge

GAUGE

12 sts and 10 rows = 4" in hdc with size J hook

BACK

- With size J hook, ch 55 (61, 67, 73), sc in 2nd ch from hook and in each ch across, turn—54 (60, 66, 72) sts. Ch 1, sc in each st across, turn. Ch 2 (count as hdc), hdc in each st across, turn.

- Set up for center panel:

  Row 1 (RS): Ch 2 (count as hdc), hdc in next 14 (17, 20, 23) sts, 2 FPdc, (4 BPdc, 4 FPdc) twice, 4 BPdc, 2 FPdc, hdc in last 15 (18, 21, 24) sts, turn.

  Row 2: Ch 2 (count as hdc), hdc in next 14 (17, 20, 23) sts, 2 BPdc, (4 FPdc, 4 BPdc) twice, 4 FPdc, 2 BPdc, hdc in last 15 (18, 21, 24) sts, turn.

Row 3: Ch 2 (count as hdc), hdc in next 14 (17, 20, 23) sts, 2 FPdc, (4 FPdc, 4 BPdc) twice, 4 FPdc, 2 FPdc, hdc in last 15 (18, 21, 24) sts, turn.

Row 4: Ch 2 (count as hdc), hdc in next 14 (17, 20, 23) sts, 2 BPdc, (4 BPdc, 4 FPdc) twice, 4 BPdc, 2 BPdc, hdc in last 15 (18, 21, 24) sts, turn.

- Rep rows 1–4 until side measures 14 (15, 15½, 16)", end with completed WS row.

- **Armhole shaping:** Sl st across next 8 (8, 9, 9) sts, ch 2 (count as dc), cont in patt across to last 7 (7, 8, 8) sts, turn. Cont in patt as established, working hdc2tog at beg and end of row on next 3 (3, 3, 3) rows—34 (40, 44, 50) sts. Cont in patt until armhole measures 8 (8, 9, 9½)", end with completed WS row.

- **Right shoulder:** Ch 2 (count as hdc), work in patt across 7 (8, 9, 11) sts, turn. Work in established patt for 1". Fasten off.

- **Left shoulder:** With RS facing, reattach yarn in st 8 (9, 10, 12) from end of row. Cont in patt for 1". Fasten off—18 (22, 24, 26) sts rem unworked in center for back neck.

FRONT

- Work as for back until armhole measures same as back and has same number of rows. End with completed WS row.

- **Left shoulder:** Ch 2 (count as hdc), work in patt across 7 (8, 9, 11) sts, turn. Cont in patt until armhole measures same as back and has same number of rows. Fasten off.

- **Right shoulder:** With RS facing, reattach yarn in st 8 (9, 10, 12) from end of row. Cont in patt until armhole measures same as back and has same number of rows. Fasten off—18 (22, 24, 26) sts rem unworked in center for front neck.

FINISHING

- Sl st shoulder seams tog.

- **Side seams:** With size J hook, sc 40 (43, 45, 49) sts evenly spaced on side edges of front and back. With WS tog, whipstitch side seams tog using chain at top of sc for even distribution of sts.

- **Neckband:** With RS facing, size I hook, and starting at right shoulder seam, sc 4 (4, 4, 4) sts to back neck, sc 18 (22, 24, 26) sts across back neck, sc 4 (4, 4, 4) sts to left shoulder seam, sc 12 (12, 15, 15) sts to front neck, sc 18 (22, 24, 26) sts across front neck, sc 12 (12, 15, 15) sts to right shoulder seam, join with sl st—68 (76, 86, 90) sts. Ch 1, sc in each st, skipping 1 st at corners, join with sl st. Fasten off. **To stabilize inside of neck:** With WS facing and size G hook, sl st tightly from

armhole across shoulder seam and back neck to opposite armhole. This will help support the weight of the garment and prevent the neck from stretching.

- **Armbands:** With RS facing, I hook, and starting at side seam, sc 8 (8, 9, 9) sts across first half of underarm sts, sc 22 (22, 25, 28) sts to shoulder seam, sc 22 (22, 25, 28) sts to underarm, sc 8 (8, 9, 9) sts across rem sts of underarm, join with sl st—60 (60, 68, 74) sts. Ch 1, sc in each st around, skipping 1 st at corners, join with sl st. Fasten off. Rep for 2nd armband.

- Lay flat. Mist with water. Lay a heavy towel over vest and allow to dry completely before removing. Do not steam or flatten patt st. Rep for other side.

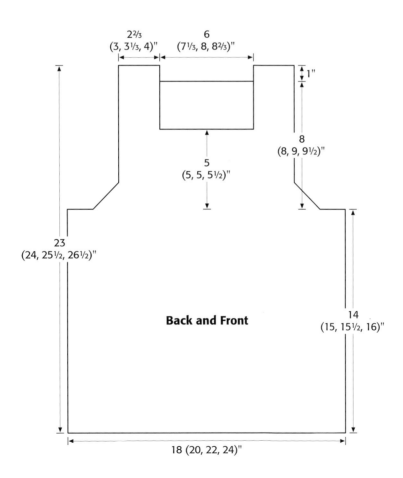

Imagination

Two unusually shaped pieces make up this vest. Each half is worked from the armhole toward the center front and the back. The back is seamed, and a border is added to the bottom edge. You'll have to keep your wits about you since the measurements are all taken from the armhole out. Follow the arrows on the schematics to help you keep your place. The vest is amazingly fun to crochet.

Skill Level: Experienced ◀■■■▶

Sizes: Small (Medium, Large, X-Large)

Finished Bust: 35½ (39½, 43, 48½)"

Finished Length: 21 (23, 25, 27)"

MATERIALS

4 (4, 5, 7) skeins of Cascade 220 by Cascade Yarns (100% wool; 100 g; 220 yds); color 9440 ⟨4⟩

G-6 (4 mm) and H-8 (5 mm) crochet hooks or size required to obtain gauge

Coilless safety pins

5 buttons, ⅞" diameter

GAUGE

16 sts and 13 rows = 4" in V-st patt with size H hook

PATTERN STITCH

Multiple of 3

(Hdc, ch 1, hdc) equals 1 V-st.

Note: Count your sts every few rows to make sure you're not leaving out any increases. It is essential that both halves contain the same number of sts in each section when they are completed.

V-Stitch Pattern

Row 1 (RS): Ch 3 (counts as hdc and ch 1), hdc in next st, *sk 2 hdc, (hdc, ch 1, hdc) in next hdc*, rep from * to * across to corner ch-1 sp with safety pin, (hdc, ch 1, hdc, ch 1, hdc, ch 1, hdc) in corner ch-1 sp, rep from * to * across to next corner ch-1 sp with safety pin, (hdc, ch 1, hdc, ch 1, hdc, ch 1, hdc) in corner ch-1 sp, rep from * to * to last 4 hdc, sk 2 hdc, (hdc, ch 1) in next hdc, hdc in tch, turn.

Row 2 (WS): Ch 3 (counts as hdc and ch 1), hdc in next ch-1 sp, (hdc, ch 1, hdc) in each ch-1 sp (including corner ch-1 sps with safety pins) to last ch-1 sp, (hdc, ch 1) in ch-1 sp, hdc in tch, turn. Move safety pin in corner ch—1 sp every few rows.

Rep rows 1 and 2 for patt.

RIGHT FRONT AND BACK

- *Starting at armhole with size H hook, ch 91 (91, 100, 102), hdc in 3rd ch from hook (count as hdc) and in next 34 (34, 37, 37) sts, (hdc, ch 1, hdc) in next ch (mark ch 1 with safety pin), hdc in next 15 (15, 18, 21) sts, (hdc, ch 1, hdc) in next ch (mark ch 1 with safety pin), hdc in 36 (36, 39, 39) sts to end—93 (93, 102, 105) sts.*

- Beg patt st, place marker in row 1 to indicate RS of back, and work until piece (shoulder) measures 3 (3½, 3½, 4)", end with completed WS row at center back.

- **Front neck (RS):** Work in patt to and including the 9 (9, 10, 10) V-st from end of row—8 (8, 9, 9) V-sts rem unworked.

- Cont in patt until back measures 7 (8, 8½, 9½)" wide. Fasten off. Set aside.

LEFT FRONT AND BACK

Note: Follow V-st Patt in first column, except row 1 will now be WS row and row 2 will now be RS row.

- Work as for right front and back from * to *.

- Beg patt st, place marker in row 2 to indicate RS of back, and work until piece (shoulder) measures 3 (3½, 3½, 4)", end with completed RS row at neck edge. There should be same number of rows and sts as right shoulder on right front. Fasten off.

- **Front neck (WS):** Reattach yarn in ch-1 sp 9 (9, 10, 10) V-sts from end of row. Cont with rem body sts as for right front and back. Fasten off. Be sure you have same number of rows and sts on both pieces.

FINISHING

- From RS, weave seam at center back.

- **Bottom border:** With RS facing, size G hook, and starting at bottom corner of left front, reattach yarn, and beg V-st patt across bottom of vest, working 1 V-st in each corner of seam at center back. Cont in patt for 3" or desired length. Fasten off.

- Weave shoulder seams tog.

- **Left front band:** With RS facing, size G hook, and starting at right front neck, (work 1 sc in each st to corner, mark last st as corner with safety pin) 4 times, sc down left front, turn. **Next 4 rows:** Ch 1, (sc in each st to 2 sts before corner, sc2tog, sc st with safety pin, sc2tog) 4 times, sc to end. AT SAME TIME, on last row, work a 2nd sc in corner of neck edge of left front and cont down left front, working 1 sc in each st to bottom border, then 2 sc in each row of bottom border, turn. **Next 5 rows:** Ch 1, sc in each st to corner of left neck. Fasten off.

- **Right front band:** With RS facing, size G hook, and starting at right front lower edge, work 2 sc in each row of bottom border and 1 sc in each st to top of neck edge. Be sure you have same number of sts as left front. **Next 4 rows:** Ch 1, sc in each st across, turn. AT SAME TIME, on row 3, work 5 buttonholes (each buttonhole is 2 sts). Place first buttonhole 12 sts up from bottom and 4 sts down from top edge (see page 21 for buttonhole calculations). **Next 5 rows:** Ch 1, sc in each st to corner of right neck. Fasten off.

- **Armbands:** With RS facing, size G hook, and starting at middle of underarm, sc in first half of underarm sts across to corner (mark last st as corner with safety pin), sc in each st around to opposite corner (mark last st as corner with safety pin), sc in rem half of underarm st, join with sl st. Ch 1, *sc in each st to 2 sts before corner, sc2tog, sc st with safety pin, sc2tog*, rep from * to * for other corner, sc in each st of underarm, join with sl st. Rep last row 2 more times. Fasten off. Rep for 2nd armband.

- Mist heavily with water. Pin corners flat. Lay towel over garment and allow to dry, or lightly steam garment.

- Sew on buttons.

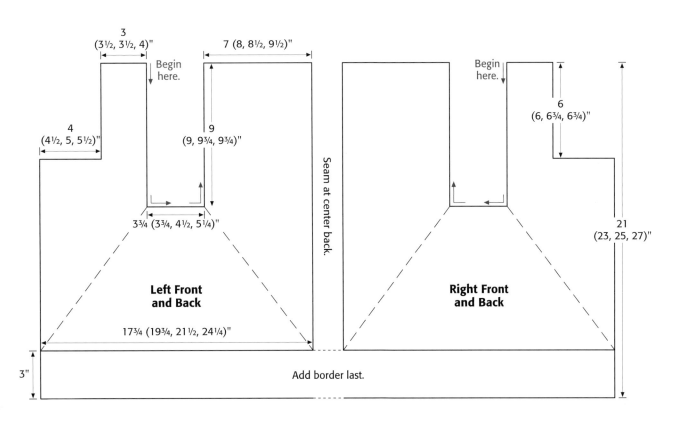

Autumn Diamonds

This simple but beautiful vest will keep you amazed and interested

as you work each diamond. Starting with one diamond unit, you crochet additional

units and partial units onto existing ones in numerical order. The color changes are

wonderful and fun. The texture of the pattern stitch gives this vest an amazing

look—you'll love every minute you're making and wearing it. ✍

Skill Level: Experienced ◖■■■▶

Sizes: Small (Medium, Large, X-Large)

Finished Bust: 35 (40, 45, 47½)"

Finished Length: 22¾ (26, 29¼, 30⅞)"

MATERIALS

2 (2, 3, 3) skeins each of Jamieson and Smith 2-ply Jumper Weight Shetland Wool
   (100% wool; 28 g; 150 yds) in the following colors:

A	FC 12	**D**	31
B	FC 38	**E**	FC 55
C	122	**F**	83

1 (1, 1, 2) skeins of Jamieson and Smith 2-ply Jumper Weight Shetland Wool,
   color FC44, for border 🧶2

D-3 (3.25 mm), E-4 (3.5 mm), and F-5 (3.75 mm) crochet hooks or size required
   to obtain gauge

5 buttons, ½" diameter

GAUGE

One diamond = 3½ (4, 4½, 4¾)" from point to point with size F hook. You must block your gauge swatch before you measure it. This yarn will soften up and the gauge will change slightly after hand washing. If you have difficulty obtaining gauge, change hook sizes or change the size you are making. The width of the vest is determined by multiplying the size of the diamond times 10. Work one bottom diamond (below) to determine gauge.

DIAMONDS

Note: Always sc through both loops at the beg and end of each row; sc in blo for the rem sts.

Bottom Diamond

With size F hook, ch 25 (29, 33, 37), sc in 2nd ch from hook, *sc in each st across, turn—24 (28, 32, 36) sts. Ch 1, sc in next 10 (12, 14, 16) sts, sc2tog twice, sc in last 10 (12, 14, 16) sts, turn. Cont on following rows, working 1 less st to center, work sc2tog twice, work 1 less st to end of row until 4 sts rem. Ch 1, sc2tog twice, turn. Ch 1, sc in 2nd st from hook. Fasten off.*

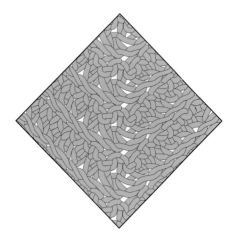

Body Diamond

With RS facing, using appropriate color according to chart, attach yarn 1 st to left of top of adjacent diamond on the right, ch 1, sc 12 (14, 16, 18) sts down left edge of diamond, sc 12 (14, 16, 18) sts up right edge of adjoining diamond, turn—24 (28, 32, 36) sts. Ch 1, work from * to * of bottom diamond.

Right Edge Half Diamond

With RS facing, using appropriate color according to chart, reattach yarn in first st at right edge of bottom diamond, ch 1, sc 14 (16, 18, 10) sts up edge of diamond, turn. **Row 1:** Ch 1, sc to last 2 sts, work sc2tog, turn. **Row 2:** Ch 1, sc2tog, work to end of row, turn. Rep these 2 rows until 2 sts rem. Ch 1, sc in 2nd st from hook. Fasten off.

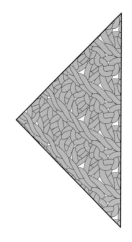

Left Edge Half Diamond

With RS facing, using appropriate color according to chart, reattach yarn in first st at top of left side of diamond, ch 1, sc 14 (16, 18, 10) sts down edge of diamond, turn. **Row 1:** Ch 1, sc2tog, work to end of row, turn. **Row 2:** Ch 1, sc to last 2 sts, sc2tog, turn. Rep these 2 rows until 2 sts rem. Ch 1, sc in 2nd st from hook. Fasten off.

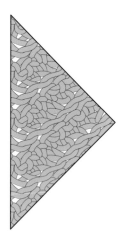

Top Half Diamond

Beg as for body diamond. Do not go to directions for bottom diamond. Ch 1, sc in each st across, turn. Work as follows:

Small

Row 1: Ch 1, sc2tog, 8 sc, sc2tog twice, 8 sc, sc2tog, turn—20 sts.

Row 2: Ch 1, sc2tog, 6 sc, sc2tog twice, 6 sc, sc2tog, turn—16 sts.

Row 3: Ch 1, sc2tog, 4 sc, sc2tog twice, 4 sc, sc2tog, turn—12 sts.

Row 4: Ch 1, sc2tog, 2 sc, sc2tog twice, 2 sc, sc2tog, turn—8 sts.

Row 5: Ch 1, sc2tog twice, turn—4 sts.

Row 6: Ch 1, sc2tog twice. Fasten off.

Medium

Row 1: Ch 1, sc2tog, 10 sc, sc2tog twice, 10 sc, sc2tog, turn—24 sts.

Cont with rows 1–6 for size Small.

Large

Row 1: Ch 1, sc2tog, 12 sc, sc2tog twice, 12 sc, sc2tog, turn—28 sts.

Row 2: Ch 1, sc2tog, 10 sc, sc2tog twice, 10 sc, sc2tog, turn—24 sts.

Cont with rows 1–6 for size Small.

X-Large

Row 1: Ch 1, sc2tog, 14 sc, sc2tog twice, 14 sc, sc2tog, turn—32 sts.

Row 2: Ch 1, sc2tog, 12 sc, sc2tog twice, 12 sc, sc2tog, turn—28 sts.

Row 3: Ch 1, sc2tog, 10 sc, sc2tog twice, 10 sc, sc2tog, turn—24 sts.

Cont with rows 1–6 for size Small.

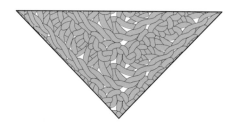

BODY

- Working from chart for color placement, make first diamond, following patt st for bottom diamond. Work rem bottom row of diamonds in order, joining new color with a sl st in left corner of last diamond made with RS facing. Ch 25 (29, 33, 37) sts and cont with patt st for bottom diamond.

- Following chart, work body diamonds and half diamonds as indicated until vest is complete.

FINISHING

- With WS facing up, weave shoulder seams tog.
- **Armbands:** With RS facing, size E hook, border color, and starting at center of under-arm, sc in next 12 (14, 16, 18) sts across each diamond edge around armhole, join with a sl st. **Next 2 rows:** Ch 1, sc into blo of each st, join with a sl st, turn. Fasten off. Rep for 2nd armband.
- **Bottom border:** Because you are working into the ch upside down, sts will appear slightly different as you look for them. With RS facing, size D hook, border color, and starting at left lower edge, ch 1, sc in next 12

(14, 16, 18) sts, * work 2 sc in each of next 2 sts (tip of point), sc in next 11 (13, 15, 17) sts, sc2tog twice (valley), sc in next 11 (13, 15, 17) sts*, rep from * to * to last point, work 2 sc in each of next 2 sts (tip of point), sc in next 12 (14, 16, 18) sts to end, turn. **Next row:** Ch 1, sc2tog, **sc in next 11 (13, 15, 17) sts, work 2 sc in each of next 2 sts (tip of point), sc in next 11 (13, 15, 17) sts, sc2tog twice (valley).** Rep from ** to **, sc in next 11 (13, 15, 17) sts, work 2 sc in each of next 2 sts (tip of point), sc in next 11 (13, 15, 17) sts, sc2tog at end of row. Fasten off.

- **Front bands and neckband:** With RS facing, size F hook, border color, and starting at lower right front edge, join yarn at lower edge of bottom border. Ch 1, work 2 sc in each st along edge of bottom border, sc in next 12 (14, 16, 18) sts on edge of each diamond, including sts of back neck diamonds, work 2 sc at points of V-necks on both fronts, 1 sc in each st around to lower edge of left front, 2 sc in each st along edge of bottom border, turn. Ch 1, sc into blo around, inc 2 sts at points of V-neck on each side.

- **Buttonhole row (RS):** Ch 1, work 3 sc, *ch 2, sk 2 sts, sc in next 10 (12, 14, 16) sts*, rep from * to * 3 more times. Ch 2, sk 2 sts, cont to sc in each st, working 2 inc at points for V-necks, turn. Ch 1, sc into blo around, work-ing 2 sc in ch-2 sp for buttonholes, turn. Ch 1, sc in blo around. Fasten off.

- Shetland yarn feels scratchy until it is wet and dried. Gently hand wash vest with a mild soap. Rinse and lay flat to dry. Shape vest to correct measurements. The yarn is fine so it will dry quickly. Do not move until dry.

- Sew on buttons.

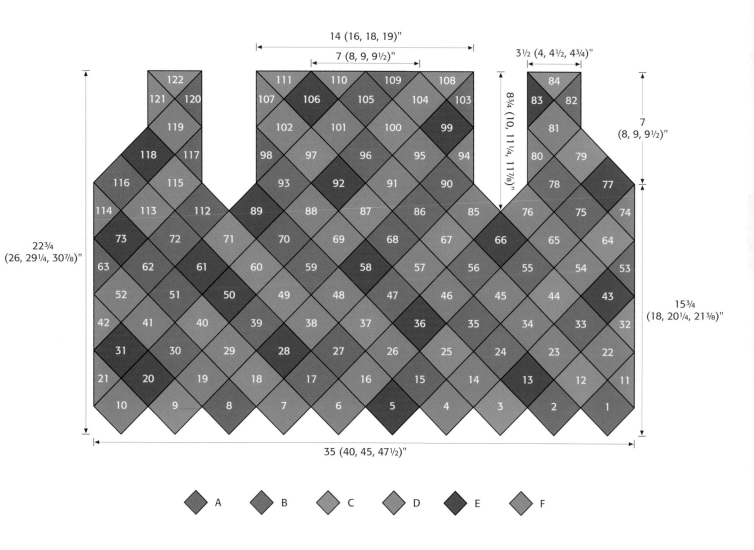

14 (16, 18, 19)"

7 (8, 9, 9½)"

3½ (4, 4½, 4¾)"

8¾ (10, 11¼, 11⅞)"

7
(8, 9, 9½)"

22¾
(26, 29¼, 30⅞)"

15¾
(18, 20¼, 21⅜)"

35 (40, 45, 47½)"

A   B   C   D   E   F

Ripples

At one time, this classic ripple pattern was most commonly used for afghans. I think

it translates beautifully into this wonderful vest in multicolored yarn. I love the way

it ripples across the body and the way the colors change as the stitches meander

up and down the hills and valleys. This was my mom's favorite pattern.

Boy, would she be surprised to see her favorite afghan pattern in this vest! 🖋

Skill Level: Intermediate ◀■■□
Sizes: Small (Medium, Large)
Finished Bust: 35 (42, 49)"
Finished Length: 22 (23, 23½)"

MATERIALS
3 (3, 4) skeins of Bearfoot by Mountain Colors (60% Superwash wool, 25% mohair, 15% nylon; 100 g; 350 yds); color Pheasant 🪶③
F-5 (3.75 mm) and G-6 (4 mm) crochet hooks or size required to obtain gauge

GAUGE
23 sts and 20 rows = 3½" wide and 4" high in patt st with size G hook when blocked

PATTERN STITCH
Multiple of 11 + 1

Foundation row (RS): Work 2 sc in 2nd ch from hook, *sc in each of next 4 ch, sk 2 ch, sc in next 4 ch, 3 sc in next ch*, rep from * to * 8 (10, 12) times, end with 1 sc in next 4 ch, sk 2 ch, sc in next 4 ch, 2 sc in last ch, turn.

Row 1: Ch 1, work 2 sc in first sc, *sc in next 4 sc, sk 2 sc, sc in next 4 sc, 3 sc in next sc*, rep from * to * 8 (10, 12) times, end with 1 sc in next 4 sc, sk 2 sc, sc in next 4 sc, 2 sc in last sc, turn.

Rep row 1 for patt.

BACK

- With size F hook, ch 112 (134, 156) sts and work foundation row—112 (134, 156) sts; 10 (12, 14) points. Work row 1 of patt st for 5 rows.

- Change to size G hook and work in patt until side measures 13 (14, 14)", end with completed WS row.

- **Armhole shaping for Small:** At beg of next row, sk 1 st, sc in next st, hdc in next 3 sts, dc in next 2 sts, hdc in next 3 sts, sl st in first st of 3 sc made in one st from previous row, work to end of row, turn. At beg of next row, sk 1 st, sc in next st, hdc in next 3 sts, dc in next 2 sts, hdc in next 3 sts, sc in next st, sl st in center st of 3 sc made in one st from previous row, cont in patt as established; turn—8 points rem. Cont in patt until armhole measures 9", end with completed WS row.

- **Armhole shaping for Medium and Large:** At beg of next row, sk 1 st, sc in next st, hdc in next 3 sts, dc in next 2 sts, hdc in next 3 sts, sl st in center st of 3 sc made in one st from previous row, sc in next st, hdc in next 3 sts, dc in next 2 sts, hdc in next 3 sts, sc in next st, sl st in first st of 3 sc made in one st from previous row, work to end of row, turn. At beg of next row, sk 1 st, *sc in next st, hdc in next 3 sts, dc in next 2 sts, hdc in next 3 sts, sc in next st, sl st in center st of 3 sc made in one st from previous row*, rep from * to * once more, cont in patt as established; turn—(8, 10) points rem. Cont in patt until armhole measures (9, 9½)", end with completed WS row.

- **Right shoulder:** Working across first 23 (23, 23) sts of patt only, sk 1 st, *sc in next st, hdc in next 3 sts, dc in next 2 sts, hdc in next 3 sts, sc in next st, sl st in center st of 3 sc made in one st from previous row*, rep from * to * once more. Change to size F hook, ch 1, sc across shoulder sts, working sc2tog 3 times evenly spaced across row, turn. Ch 1, sc in each st across. Fasten off.

- **Left shoulder:** With RS facing, reattach yarn in center st of 3 sc made in one st from previous row at top of second point from left. *Sc in next st, hdc in next 3 sts, dc in next 2 sts, hdc in next 3 sts, sc in next st, sl st in center st of 3 sc made in one st from previous row*, rep from * to * once more. Change to size F hook, ch 1, sc across shoulder sts, working sc2tog 3 times evenly across row, turn. Ch 1, sc in each st across. Fasten off—4 (4, 6) points rem in center for back neck.

FRONT

- Work as for back until armhole measures 5½ (5½, 6)".

- **Left shoulder:** Work across first 23 (23, 23) sts of patt, turn. Cont in patt until armhole measures 9 (9, 9½)". Work shoulder shaping as for back right shoulder.

- **Right shoulder:** With RS facing, reattach yarn in center st of 3 sc made in one st from previous row at top of 2nd point from left. Work across last 23 sts only, turn. Cont in patt until armhole measures 9 (9, 9½)". Work shoulder shaping as for back left shoulder. Fasten off—4 (4, 6) points rem in center for front neck.

FINISHING

- Sl st shoulder seams tog.
- Weave side seams tog.
- **Armbands:** With RS facing, size F hook, and starting at underarm seam, work (2 sc, sk 1 st) across to armhole edge, 1 sc in each row around armhole to underarm, (2 sc, sk 1 st) for rem sts of underarm, join with a sl st. Ch 1, work (2 sc, sk 1 st) across first half of underarm sts and 1 sc in each sc for rem sleeve opening around to underarm, work (2 sc, sk 1 st) for rem half of underarm, join with a sl st. Fasten off. Rep for 2nd armband.

- **Neckband:** With RS facing, size F hook, and working across straight edge along sides of neck, work 1 sc for each row from back neck to front neck for right shoulder, and from front neck to back neck for left shoulder. Fasten off.

- Heavily mist with water and lay flat to dry. You may find that you'll need to gently steam the points to make them lie flat. You can steam the entire vest so that it lies perfectly flat, or you can allow the knitted fabric to form ripples if you desire. The more you steam the vest, the less the ripples will show.

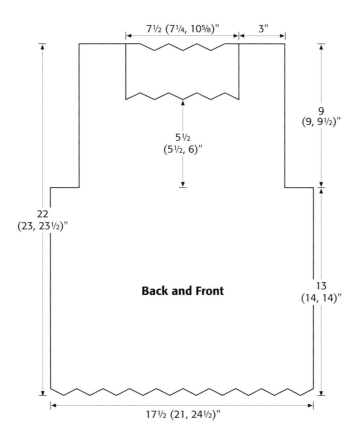

Waffles

This pattern stitch looks and feels just like a waffle—the texture is fabulous.

The stitch is simple to do but fascinating to work. The vest makes me think

of a Sunday morning out to breakfast with all the trimmings:

butter, syrup, and powdered sugar, not to mention the coffee.

This is a fun stitch that makes a versatile vest. 🐚

Skill Level: Intermediate ◼◼◼▢

Sizes: Small (Medium, Large, X-Large, XX-Large)

Finished Bust: 34½ (39½, 42½, 46½, 50½)"

Finished Length: 21¾ (22¼, 23¼, 24¼, 25¼)"

MATERIALS

7 (8, 9, 11, 13) skeins of Merino DK by Debbie Bliss (100% merino wool; 50 g; 110 m); color 702

G-6 (4 mm) crochet hook or size required to obtain gauge

Coilless safety pins

GAUGE

16 sts and 16 rows = 4" in patt st

PATTERN STITCH

Multiple of 2 plus 1

Foundation row (RS): Sk first ch next to hook, *insert hook in next ch and pull up a loop, insert hook in next ch and pull up a loop, YO, draw through 2 loops, YO, draw through last 2 loops, ch 1, rep from * to last ch, sc in last ch, turn.

Row 1: Ch 1, *insert hook under next st before vertical strand of yarn from row below and pull up a loop, insert hook under st after vertical strand of yarn and pull up a loop, YO, draw through 2 loops, YO, draw through last 2 loops on hook, ch 1, rep from * to last st, sc in last st, turn.

Rep row 1 for patt.

BACK

- *Ch 70 (80, 86, 94, 102) sts and work foundation row—69 (79, 85, 93, 101) sts. Work row 1 of patt st until side measures 12 (12½, 13, 13½, 14)", end with completed WS row.

- **Armhole shaping:** Sl st across 9 (11, 13, 13, 15) sts, ch 1, cont in patt to last 8 (10, 12, 12, 14) sts, turn—53 (59, 61, 69, 73) sts.* On next 2 rows, work dec at beg and end of row as follows: Sk first 2 sts (st before and after first vertical strand of yarn), cont in patt to 2 sts from end of row (st before and after last vertical strand of yarn), sk these 2 sts, sc in tch (4 sts decreased on each row)—45 (51, 53, 61, 65) sts. Cont in patt until armhole measures 9 (9, 9½, 10, 10½)", end with completed WS row.

- **Right shoulder:** Work in patt across first 10 (11, 12, 14, 16) sts, turn. Work 1 more row in patt. Fasten off.

- **Left shoulder:** With RS facing, reattach yarn in st 10 (11, 12, 14, 16) from end of row, ch 1, work in patt to end of row, turn. Work 1 more row in patt. Fasten off—25 (29, 29, 33, 33) sts rem unworked in center for back neck.

FRONT

- Work as for back from * to *. With RS facing, place a safety pin in st 27 (30, 31, 35, 37) to mark center st.

- **Left armhole and neck shaping:** On next 2 rows, dec at armhole edge as follows: **Row 1:** Sk first 2 sts (st before and after first vertical strand of yarn) and cont in patt to safety pin, turn (2 sts dec). **Row 2:** Work in patt to 2 sts from end of row (st before and after last vertical strand of yarn), sk these 2 sts, sc in tch (2 sts dec), and AT SAME TIME work dec at neck edge as described in row 2 above on every 4th row 6 (7, 7, 8, 8) times—10 (11, 12, 14, 16) sts. When armhole measures same as back, fasten off.

- **Right armhole and neck shaping:** With RS facing, reattach yarn 1 st to left of safety pin, ch 1, cont in patt to end of row, turn. Work as for left armhole and neck, reversing shaping.

FINISHING

- Weave shoulder seams and side seams tog.
- **Neckband:** With RS facing and starting at right shoulder seam, sc 3 (3, 3, 3, 3) sts to back neck, sc 27 (29, 31, 35, 35) sts across back neck, sc 3 (3, 3, 3, 3) sts to left shoulder seam, sc 32 (32, 34, 36, 38) sts to safety pin, sk st with safety pin, sc 32 (32, 34, 36, 38) sts to right shoulder seam, join with sl st—97 (99, 105, 113, 117) sts. Work foundation row of patt st, except join with a sl st instead of sc in st at end of row. Ch 1, work row 1 of patt, sk st at safety pin, join with sl st at end of row. Fasten off.

- **Armbands:** With RS facing and starting at underarm seam, sc 8 (10, 12, 12, 14) sts across first half of underarm, sc 35 (35, 37, 39, 41) sts to shoulder seam, sc 1 (1, 1, 1, 1) st at shoulder seam, sc 35 (35, 37, 39, 41) sts to lower edge of underarm, sc 8 (10, 12, 12, 14) sts in each rem st of underarm, join with sl st—87 (91, 99, 103, 111) sts. Work foundation row of patt st, except join with sl st instead of sc in st at end of row. Ch 1, work row 1 of patt, join with a sl st at end of row. Fasten off. Rep for 2nd armband.

- Mist with water and lay flat to dry. Do not flatten patt st.

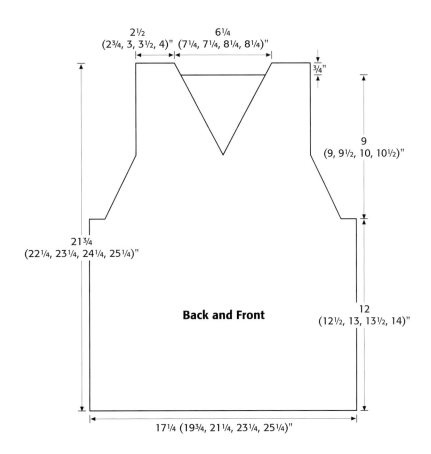

2½
(2¾, 3, 3½, 4)"

6¼
(7¼, 7¼, 8¼, 8¼)"

¾"

9
(9, 9½, 10, 10½)"

21¾
(22¼, 23¼, 24¼, 25¼)"

Back and Front

12
(12½, 13, 13½, 14)"

17¼ (19¾, 21¼, 23¼, 25¼)"

Madelaine

The name of this yarn reminds me of wonderful French cookies called madeleines.

They are buttery soft and sweet and made in a mold that resembles an elongated

seashell. I love them with tea. This yarn, with a similar name to the cookie, is just as

soft and wonderful as butter as it runs through your fingers. I wanted a delicate

pattern that would equal the softness of the yarn. Your job is to find just the right

outfit to wear it with. How about with a flowered spring dress to go to a tea salon? 🍂

Skill Level: Intermediate ◼◼◼▭
Sizes: Small (Medium, Large, X-Large)
Finished Bust: 38¾ (42, 47¼, 51)"
Finished Length: 21 (22½, 24, 24½)"

MATERIALS

6 (8, 10, 12) skeins of Madelaine by Knit One, Crochet Too (100% superfine
   merino wool; 50 g; 198 yds [181 m]); color 415 **2**
D-3 (3.25 mm) and E-4 (3.5 mm) crochet hooks or size required to obtain gauge
Coilless safety pins
6 buttons, ⅜" diameter

GAUGE

22 sts and 17 rows = 4" in shell patt st with size E hook
For gauge swatch: Ch 23, sc in 2nd ch from hook and in each st across, turn.
Follow shell patt st.

PATTERN STITCHES
Shell Pattern Stitch
Multiple of 4 plus 2

Row 1 (RS): Ch 2 (count as dc), sk 1 st, work 4 dc in next st, *sk 3 sts, work 4 dc in next st, rep from * to last 3 sts, sk 2 sts, work 2 dc in last st, turn.

Rows 2, 4, 6, and 8: Ch 1 (does not count as st), sc in each st across, turn.

Rows 3 and 7: Ch 2 (count as dc), dc in each st across, turn.

Row 5: Ch 2 (count as dc), work 1 dc in same st as ch 2, 4 dc in next st, *sk 3 sts, work 4 dc in next st, rep from * to last 6 sts, sk 3 sts, work 3 dc in next st, sk 1 st, work 1 dc in last st, turn.

Rep rows 1–8 for patt.

Yoke Pattern
Row 1 (RS): Ch 2 (count as dc), dc in each st across, turn.

Row 2: Ch 1 (does not count as st), sc in each st across, turn.

Rep rows 1 and 2 for patt.

BACK
- **Bottom border:** With size E hook, ch 99 (109, 121, 133) sts, sc in 2nd ch from hook and in each st across, turn—98 (108, 120, 132) sts. **Next 3 rows:** Ch 1, sc in each st across, turn. **Next row:** Ch 2 (count as dc), dc in each st across, turn. **Next row:** Ch 1, sc in each st across, turn. **Next row:** Ch 1, sc in each st across, inc 8 (10, 10, 10) sts evenly spaced, turn—106 (118, 130, 142) sts.

- Beg shell patt st and work until side measures 12 (13, 14, 14½)", end with completed WS row 2, 4, 6, or 8.

- **Armhole shaping:** Sl st across next 15 (17, 19, 21) sts, work row 1 of yoke patt to last 14 (16, 18, 20) sts, turn. Cont in yoke patt, working a dc2tog or a sc2tog, depending on what row

you are on, at beg and end of next 6 (7, 9, 11) rows—66 (72, 76, 80) sts. Cont in yoke patt until armhole measures 9 (9½, 10, 10)", end with completed WS row. Fasten off. Place a safety pin in st 15 (16, 18, 18) from each armhole edge to mark shoulders.

LEFT FRONT
- *Ch 51 (55, 63, 67) sts, work bottom border as for back, except inc 4 sts on last row of border instead of 8—54 (58, 66, 70) sts. Beg shell patt st and work until side measures 12 (13, 14, 14½)", end with completed WS row 2, 4, 6, or 8 (should be the same row you ended on for the back).*

- **Armhole and neck shaping:** Sl st across next 15 (17, 19, 21) sts, work row 1 of yoke patt across row, turn. Cont in yoke patt, working a dc2tog or a sc2tog, depending on what row you are on, at armhole edge on next 6 (7, 9, 11) rows. AT SAME TIME beg neck shaping: On back, count 20 (20, 22, 22) rows down from shoulder. Mark row with safety pin. When you reach that row as you work front, work a sc2tog or a dc2tog, depending on what row you are on, at neck edge on next 19 (19, 21, 21) rows. You should have 1 row rem without a dec; be sure it is the same row the back ended with—15 (16, 18, 18) sts. When armhole measures 9 (9½, 10, 10)", fasten off.

RIGHT FRONT
- Work as for left front from * to *.

- **Armhole and neck shaping:** Work row 1 of yoke patt to last 14 (16, 18, 20) sts, turn. Cont in yoke patt, working a dc2tog or a sc2tog, depending on what row you are on, at armhole edge on next 6 (7, 9, 11) rows. AT SAME TIME beg neck shaping on same row as neck shaping on left front. Cont in yoke patt and finish as for left front—15 (16, 18, 18) sts. Fasten off.

FINISHING

- Sl st shoulder seams tog.
- Weave side seams tog.
- **Collar:** With RS of right front facing, size E hook, and starting at first dec of neck shaping, ch 1, work 1 sc in sc rows and 2 sc in dc rows to shoulder seam, sc 31 (35, 35, 39) sts across back neck, and again 1 sc in sc rows and 2 sc in dc rows to start of left front neck shaping, turn. Be sure there are the same number of sts for collar on both fronts. **Next row:** Ch 1, sc in each st around neck edge, turn. **Next row:** Count sts before you work this row because you need to have a multiple of 4 plus 2; in other words, the number of sts should divide evenly by 4 with 2 left over. If they don't, dec as needed on back neck of this row. Ch 1, sc in each st around neck edge, turn. See box below.

Work the following 2 rows until collar measures 4 (4¼, 4½, 4¾)", end with completed WS row.

Row 1 (WS): Ch 1, sc in each st across, turn.

Row 2: Ch 2 (count as st), dc in same st as ch 2, *sk 3 sts, work 4 dc in next st, rep from * to last 6 sts, sk 3 sts, work 3 dc in next st, sk 1 st, work 1 dc in last st, turn.

Work 4 rows of row 1. Fasten off.

Finding the Correct Number of Stitches for Pattern Multiple

When you work with a pattern that has a multiple, you must have the correct number of stitches in which to work the multiple. It's easy math, but you don't want to use a calculator because you need to have whole numbers, not fractions, if you are going to have a remainder. For the shell stitch pattern, the multiple is 4 plus 2. Without the 2 extra stitches, the pattern won't end correctly at the end of the row. You'll need to work this out for the collar on the vest, since I can't tell you how many stitches you'll have when you are finished working the first row of single crochet around the neck (it depends on your individual gauge). Here is the basic math to help you find the correct number of stitches for the collar to work with the pattern multiple of 4 plus 2.

Example:
Let's say you have 136 stitches after the first row of single crochet around the neck. So 136 divided by 4 equals 34 repeats with no stitches remaining. But you need to have 2 extra stitches to accommodate the "plus 2" of the multiple. To make the pattern multiple of 4 plus 2 work, you need to get to 134 stitches. To do this, simply decrease 2 stitches at the back neck. The 134 stitches divided by 4 equals 33 repeats plus 2 stitches left over.

Using the numbers you have, fill in the blanks:
Number of stitches you have (__) divided by 4 equals ___ repeats with a remainder of __. If the remainder is 2, you're all set. If the remainder is anything but 2, you have to decrease at back neck to make sure it comes out to 2. The reason you are decreasing at the back neck is to keep the collar the same size on the right and left fronts.

- **Armbands:** With RS facing, size E hook, and starting at underarm seam, ch 1, sc in first half of underarm sts, mark last st as corner with safety pin, work 2 sc in each dc row, 1 sc in each sc row around armhole to underarm, mark last st as corner with safety pin, work 1 sc in each st of rem underarm sts, join with a sl st. Change to size D hook. (Ch 1, sc in each st around, skipping 1 st in corners, join with a sl st) twice. Fasten off. Rep for 2nd armband.

- **Left front band:** With RS facing, size E hook, and starting at point of collar, ch 1, work 1 sc in sc rows and 2 sc in dc rows to bottom edge of front. Change to size D hook. **Next 4 rows:** Ch 1, sc in each st across, turn. Fasten off.

- **Right front band:** With RS facing, size E hook, and starting at lower edge, work as for left front. Be sure you have same number of sts as left front. Ch 1, work 1 more row sc. Work 6 buttonholes in next row. Each buttonhole is 2 sts and there are 6 sts at bottom before buttonholes start (see page 21 to calculate buttonhole placement). Place the last buttonhole before the start of the V-neck shaping. Follow buttonhole row with 2 more rows of sc. Fasten off.

- Heavily mist, lay flat, pin out points, and allow to dry. You may need to rep for other side. Yarn may be steamed to tame points of collar and fronts.

- Sew on buttons.

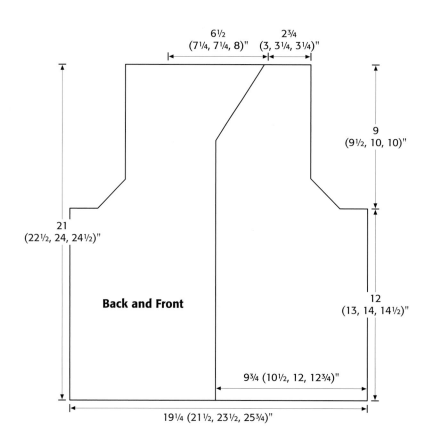

6½
(7¼, 7¼, 8)"

2¾
(3, 3¼, 3¼)"

9
(9½, 10, 10)"

21
(22½, 24, 24½)"

Back and Front

12
(13, 14, 14½)"

9¾ (10½, 12, 12¾)"

19¼ (21½, 23½, 25¾)"

Resources

I give many thanks to the following yarn companies for generously supplying the yarn for this book. For a list of shops in your area or mail-order and Internet companies that carry the yarns in this book, write to the companies below or visit their Web sites.

Berroco, Inc.
PO Box 367
Uxbridge, MA 01569-0367
www.berroco.com

Cascade Yarns
PO Box 58168
Tukwila, WA 98138-1168
www.cascadeyarns.com

Crystal Palace
160 23rd St.
Richmond, CA 94804-1812
www.straw.com

Dale of Norway
N16 W23390 Stoneridge Dr., Ste. A
Waukesha, WI 53188
www.dale.no

JCA, Inc.
35 Scales Ln.
Townsend, MA 01469-1094
Distributor of Reynolds yarns.

Knitting Fever, Inc.
35 Debevoise Ave.
Roosevelt, NY 11575-1171
www.knittingfever.com
Distributor of Noro and Debbie Bliss yarns.

Knit One, Crochet Too
7 Commons Ave, Ste. 2
Windham, ME 04062
www.knitonecrochettoo.com

Skacel Collection, Inc.
PO Box 88110
Seattle, WA 98168
www.skacelknitting.com

Jamieson and Smith
9 North Rd.
Lerwick, Shetland Isles ZE1 OPQ
011 44 1595 6935 79
This yarn is available in many stores in the United States. For mail order, call the phone number listed above.

Mountain Colors
PO Box 156
Corvallis, MT 59828
www.mountaincolors.com

Trendsetter Yarns
16745 Saticoy St. #101
Van Nuys, CA 97406

About the Author

In 1987, while still working as a registered nurse, Nancie Wiseman opened a yarn shop called Nancie Knits in Sacramento, California. This started Nancie on a dynamic career as a popular designer of, and nationally known teacher of, knitted and crocheted garments. She has designed patterns for top yarn companies, including Cascade Yarns, Prism, Lorna's Laces, Rainbow Mills, and Trendsetter Yarns. Her articles and designs have been published in *Interweave Knits, Knit 'n Style, Knitter's Magazine*, and *Piecework*. Nancie was also a consultant and designer for a "Knitting 101" article in *Martha Stewart Living* and contributed to the DVD *The Art of Knitting*. She's appeared on the DIY Network's *Jewelry Making Show* on cable television and the *Shay Pendray Needlearts Studio* on PBS. In 1995, Nancie started the production company Wisewater Productions, and it has produced seven bestselling videos.

Nancie's books include *Knitted Shawls, Stoles, and Scarves* (Martingale & Company, 2001), *The Knitter's Book of Finishing Techniques* (Martingale & Company, 2002), and *Classic Knitted Vests* (Martingale & Company, 2003).

Nancie lives on Whidbey Island, Washington, in the quaint town of Coupeville with her husband, Bill Attwater, and their dogs, Amber, a golden retriever, and Pumpkin, a Yorkie.

New and Bestselling Titles from

Martingale & COMPANY

America's Best-Loved Craft & Hobby Books®
America's Best-Loved Knitting Books®

America's Best-Loved Quilt Books®

NEW RELEASES

300 Paper-Pieced Quilt Blocks
American Doll Quilts
Classic Crocheted Vests
Dazzling Knits
Follow-the-Line Quilting Designs
Growing Up with Quilts
Hooked on Triangles
Knitting with Hand-Dyed Yarns
Lavish Lace
Layer by Layer
Lickety-Split Quilts
Magic of Quiltmaking, The
More Nickel Quilts
More Reversible Quilts
No-Sweat Flannel Quilts
One-of-a-Kind Quilt Labels
Patchwork Showcase
Pieced to Fit
Pillow Party!
Pursenalities
Quilter's Bounty
Quilting with My Sister
Seasonal Quilts Using Quick Bias
Two-Block Appliqué Quilts
Ultimate Knitted Tee, The
Vintage Workshop, The
WOW! Wool-on-Wool Folk-Art Quilts

KNITTING

Basically Brilliant Knits
Beyond Wool
Classic Knitted Vests
Comforts of Home
Dazzling Knits **NEW!**
Fair Isle Sweaters Simplified
Garden Stroll, A
Knit it Now!
Knits for Children and Their Teddies
Knits from the Heart
Knitted Shawls, Stoles, and Scarves
Knitted Throws and More
Knitter's Book of Finishing Techniques, The
Knitter's Template, A
Knitting with Hand-Dyed Yarns **NEW!**
Knitting with Novelty Yarns
Lavish Lace **NEW!**
Little Box of Scarves, The
Little Box of Sweaters, The
More Paintbox Knits

Pursenalities **NEW!**
Simply Beautiful Sweaters
Simply Beautiful Sweaters for Men
Style at Large
Too Cute!
Treasury of Rowan Knits, A
Ultimate Knitted Tee, The **NEW!**
Ultimate Knitter's Guide, The

CROCHET

Classic Crocheted Vests **NEW!**
Crochet for Babies and Toddlers
Crochet for Tots
Crocheted Aran Sweaters
Crocheted Lace
Crocheted Socks!
Crocheted Sweaters
Today's Crochet

CRAFTS

20 Decorated Baskets
Beaded Elegance
Blissful Bath, The
Collage Cards
Creating with Paint
Holidays at Home
Pretty and Posh
Purely Primitive
Stamp in Color
Trashformations
Warm Up to Wool
Year of Cats...in Hats!, A

APPLIQUÉ

Appliquilt in the Cabin
Blossoms in Winter
Garden Party
Shadow Appliqué
Stitch and Split Appliqué
Sunbonnet Sue All through the Year

LEARNING TO QUILT

101 Fabulous Rotary-Cut Quilts
Happy Endings, Revised Edition
Loving Stitches, Revised Edition
More Fat Quarter Quilts
Quilter's Quick Reference Guide, The
Sensational Settings, Revised Edition
Simple Joys of Quilting, The
Your First Quilt Book (or it should be!)

PAPER PIECING

40 Bright and Bold Paper-Pieced Blocks
50 Fabulous Paper-Pieced Stars
Down in the Valley
Easy Machine Paper Piecing
For the Birds
Papers for Foundation Piecing
Quilter's Ark, A
Show Me How to Paper Piece
Traditional Quilts to Paper Piece

QUILTS FOR BABIES & CHILDREN

Easy Paper-Pieced Baby Quilts
Easy Paper-Pieced Miniatures
Even More Quilts for Baby
More Quilts for Baby
Quilts for Baby
Sweet and Simple Baby Quilts

ROTARY CUTTING/SPEED PIECING

365 Quilt Blocks a Year Perpetual
    Calendar
1000 Great Quilt Blocks
Burgoyne Surrounded
Clever Quarters
Clever Quilts Encore
Endless Stars
Once More around the Block
Pairing Up
Stack a New Deck
Star-Studded Quilts
Strips and Strings
Triangle-Free Quilts

Our books are available at
bookstores and your favorite
craft, fabric, and yarn retailers.
If you don't see the title
you're looking for, visit us at
www.martingale-pub.com
or contact us at:

1-800-426-3126

International: 1-425-483-3313
Fax: 1-425-486-7596
Email: info@martingale-pub.com